UNEXPLAINED

CONTROVERSIAL

SHATTERING R

LEARN THE STARTLING FACTS
SCIENTISTS KNOW BUT WON'T TELL YOU . . .

* The mysterious ancient seaport city found
. . . high in the Andes Mountains!

* The amazing discovery found in Antarctica
. . . in a meteorite from Mars

* The uncanny secrets known to the primitive
Dogon tribe of Africa . . . provided by a
"god from the heavens"

* The ancient "hieroglyphic writing" found carved on
a coal mine wall . . . in Hammondville, Ohio!

* The wooden model of a modern jetliner discovered
hidden . . . in an Egyptian tomb

And more, including—

* The truth about the mysterious Face on Mars!

MARTIAN GENESIS

BY THE SAME AUTHOR

Ancient Spirit
Aquarian Guide to the New Age (with Eileen Campbell)
Astral Doorways
Discover Astral Projection
Discover Reincarnation
Experimental Magic
Getting Rich: A Beginner's Manual
A Guide to Megalithic Ireland
How to Get Where You Want to Go
Magick for Beginners
Mindreach
Nostradamus—Visions of the Future
An Occult History of the World
Occult Reich
Reincarnation
Time Travel: A New Perspective
The Ultimate Elsewhere

MARTIAN
GENESIS

THE EXTRATERRESTRIAL ORIGINS
OF THE HUMAN RACE

HERBIE
BRENNAN

A DELL BOOK

Published by
Dell Publishing
a division of
Random House, Inc.
1540 Broadway
New York, New York 10036

Cover design by Gerald Pfeifer

For information, address Delacorte Press, New York,
New York.

The trademark Dell® is registered in the U.S. Patent and
Trademark Office.

ISBN: 0-440-23557-X

Reprinted by arrangement with Judy Piatkus
(Publishers) Ltd., 5 Windmill Street, London W1P 1HF

Printed in the United States of America

Published simultaneously in Canada

April 2000

10 9 8 7 6 5 4 3 2

OPM

TO CHRIS AND BRIDGET,
WITH LOVE

CONTENTS

1	The Face on Mars	1
2	Life, But Not As We Know It?	10
3	Ancestral Contact	21
4	Signs of Visitors	32
5	In the Myths of Time	40
6	Paradise Lost	47
7	A Mysterious Map	53
8	Phoenix Rising	59
9	Worshiping the Goddess	71
10	Astronomer Priests	77
11	Moving Mountains	84
12	Temples to the Stars	95
13	The Pyramid Mystery	105
14	The Port in the Sky	114
15	Shaping the Stones	126
16	Science of the Ancient World	137
17	The Restless Earth	151
18	Egypt and Israel	158
19	A Dangerous Artifact	169
20	Chinese Conundrum	183
21	Ancient Aircraft	201
22	Martian Seed	215
	Epilogue	230
	Index	235

1 | THE FACE ON MARS

IN JUNE 1976, NASA space probe, *Viking I*, went into orbit around the planet Mars. Just under two months later, a second probe—*Viking II*—was put in place. These two craft undertook a massive photographic survey of the Martian surface.

Among some 60,000 pictures returned by the orbiters, eighteen were taken at 40.9° North latitude, 9.45° West longitude, a region known as Cydonia Mensae. Five of the eighteen showed a curious rock formation that looked like a human face. The best of these photographs received widespread press coverage. The rock formation was dubbed the "Face on Mars."

Three years after the pictures were returned, independent experts began seriously to analyze the NASA images of the Cydonia region. They were interested not only in the "Face" but in several other nearby features of an unusual nature. In 1993, a group of highly respected academics from the United States and Sweden endorsed a report by Professor Stanley V. McDaniel[1] on the Martian anomalies.

The report presented evidence that the "Face" was artificial.

---

[1] Professor Emeritus and former Chairman, Dept. of Philosophy, Sonoma State University, California.

2

INIS TUAISCEART, the northernmost of the Blasket Islands off the southwest coast of Ireland, is colloquially known as An Fear Marbh, the Dead Man. The reason for this curious name is that the island's rock formations give it the appearance of a corpse laid out for burial.[2] Although the resemblance is striking, there has yet to be any suggestion it is artificial. The Dead Man is nothing more than the result of natural weathering and erosion.

The distinguished astronomer and expert in extraterrestrial intelligence, Professor Frank Drake, thinks the "Face on Mars" is something of that sort. Like the "Man in the Moon," it's "just an accident of topography and photography."[3] NASA took much the same view when the images were first released. Official statements dismissed the "Face" as a trick of light and shade created by the way sunlight struck a natural rock formation. But Professor McDaniel isn't so sure. He has problems with the fact that the two best *Viking* images of the "Face" were taken at different angles of the sun (10° and 27°). They were also taken with different camera angles, satellite altitude and orbital inclination. He argues that if the "Face" was a trick of the light, it should have disappeared—or at least distorted—when the light changed. Professor McDaniel doesn't think the "Face" is a trick of the light. He thinks it's a face and he believes it may be artificial. There are other experts who agree with him.

---

[2] A prominent bulge at the genital area has prompted a local variation of The Dead Bishop.

[3] In a footnote to the book *Is Anyone Out There?* by Frank Drake and Dava Sobel, Simon & Schuster Ltd., London, 1993.

3

PHOTOCLINOMETRY IS A TECHNIQUE developed by astronomers to help analyze the topography of the moon. Essentially it estimates the shape of an object from the relative degrees of light and shade in a photograph—shape from shading. Dr. Mark Carlotto, an authority on digital image processing based at the Analytic Sciences Corporation in Boston, Massachusetts, applied the technique to the *Viking* photographs. Not only was he able to work out a consistent three-dimensional structure from both the main images of the "Face," but he was able to *predict* the appearance of each image (at their differing sun angles) by analyzing the other. He concluded:

> The features are present in the underlying topography and do seem to reflect recognizably facial characteristics over a wide range of illumination conditions and perspectives.[4]

In other words, what seems to be a face in the photographs is actually a face on the ground. It's not, as Professor Drake claims, an illusion like the "Man in the Moon."

4

THIS DOESN'T MEAN it can't be a natural formation like Inis Tuaisceart, or the Old Man of the Mountain, a face-like rock in New Hampshire.

But both Inis Tuaisceart and the Old Man of the Mountain have human features *in profile*. To achieve a profile likeness, you only need an outline. A full-face

---

[4] Quoted from *The McDaniel Report* compiled by Stanley V. McDaniel, North Atlantic Books, Berkeley, California, 1993.

likeness is more complex. A full-face *three-dimensional* likeness—as revealed by photoclinometry—is more sophisticated still. There is not a single known example of such a natural formation anywhere on Earth, the moon, or even Mars if we ignore the "Face" itself.

Just how good a representation of the human face exists on Mars is underlined by studies of the photographs. When you first look at the most widely published of the NASA images, what you see is an eye-socket, the outline of a nose and a portion of a mouth. The left-hand side of the "Face" (to the right of the picture as you look at it) is in shadow. The whole thing is partly framed by some sort of platform that looks like a helmet.

But this image is the result of a digital transmission. Digital cameras on orbiting spacecraft encode data received from their subjects and transmit this encoded data back to base. First interpretation of the data gives the broad outlines of the subject photographed. Computer enhancement is needed to extract the fine detail. This is done not by any form of retouching or guesswork, but by statistically recovering the data used to create each individual pixel of the original. It is a standard approach to interpreting broadcast photographs from space.

Under computer enhancement, it has been shown that the "helmet" of the "Face on Mars" is decorated with evenly spaced diagonal stripes. There is a crescent diadem on the forehead made from crossed lines at the exact axis of symmetry. There are teeth in the mouth. All these features appear in both the main *Viking* images, so they are not random artifacts created by radio interference or anything of that sort. The eye, under contrast control, reveals a brow, an eyelid, and a raised pupil outlined in contour lines.

On the shadow side of the "Face," computer enhancement shows the headpiece continues around to frame the head. The line of the mouth also continues.

There is a second eye socket just where you would expect one to be. Computer reconstruction of the 3-D "Face" shows three-dimensional symmetry.

This level of detail more or less rules out the possibility that the "Face" was formed by wind erosion. As a natural feature, each of its elements would have to be explained by a wholly different geological rationale.

5

JAMES L. ERJAVEC is a geologist and computer/geographic information system analyst with more than thirteen years experience. He has developed an extensive feature map of the Cydonia region of Mars to assist in the establishment of a geologic baseline for continued studies. Erjavec does not believe *any* of the curious features at Cydonia can be the work of wind erosion.

In a paper published in 1996, he pointed out that the theory of erosion is based on the premise that the Martian northern lowland plains were once covered with a kilometer or more of erodible sediment. But in 1989, geologist G. E. McGill used crater dimensional equations to conclude that only a slight to modest erosion of the northern lowland plains could have occurred. At best, no more than 200 meters of material could have been stripped off the plains. This is simply not enough to allow the development of the Cydonia structures through erosion.

6

IF YOU UNDERTAKE art training, you learn the classical proportions of the human face—how the distance from chin to nose relates to the distance between eyebrow and hairline, where eyes or ears should be placed and so on.

The artist and anthropologist James Channon examined the "Face on Mars" and found its proportions were in accord with the classical canons. He concluded that the structure was ". . . a consciously created monument typical of the archaeology left . . . by our predecessor."[5] Channon thinks the "Face" is an artwork.

7

FRACTALS ARE GEOMETRIC figures characterized by something called self-similarity. This means that any area of the figure is a smaller copy of a larger portion.

Fractal geometry is something relatively new—it was introduced as recently as 1975—but has already influenced scientific disciplines as diverse as chemistry, physiology, and fluid mechanics. Fractal analysis is based on the discovery that natural terrain tends to follow the rules of fractal mathematics, while artificial constructs do not. If you run a fractal analysis of a natural object and graph the results, the typical "signature" is a straight line. With an artifact, the signature is curved.

These two facts allow you to estimate the probability that you're dealing with an artifact. The more curved the signature, the more likely the object is to be artificial. When used to evaluate satellite photographs of the Earth's surface, fractal analysis is 80 percent accurate in identifying man-made objects.

Dr. Carlotto and his colleague Michael C. Stein applied fractal analysis to the "Face on Mars." It gave them much the same curve you'd find on the fractal analysis of a Jeep.

---

[5] Quoted from *The McDaniel Report*.

8

CYDONIA MENSAE is a region of buttes and mesas along an escarpment separating heavily cratered southern highlands from the lowland plains to the north. Apart from the "Face," it has a number of structures unlike anything seen elsewhere on Mars.

When Dr. Carlotto ran a full fractal analysis of the area, three of them generated the curved signature typical of artificial constructs.

9

IN 1993, the award-winning architect Robert Fiertek completed a four-year study of the Mars structures that included careful measurements of their relative alignments. He was so impressed by their architectural symmetries that he concluded:

> It can be argued that individual objects at Cydonia may or may not be artificial, but it is *very* doubtful that the complex as a whole is anything but artificial.[6]

Several of the structures appear pyramidal in shape. One of them, discovered in 1980 by Vincent DiPietro and Gregory Molenaar, is now usually referred to as the D&M Pyramid in their honor. It is five-sided and symmetrical, apart from what appears to be impact damage on its eastern side. In 1988, the geographer and cartographer Erol Toron undertook the geometrical reconstruction of the pyramid's original shape. During the course of this project he attempted to discover the nat-

---

[6] Quoted from *The McDaniel Report*.

ural process that would account for the observed characteristics of the structure.

There are five recognized possibilities: liquid flow, volcanic action, wind erosion, gravity, and crystal growth, although the last of these would generally be considered a most unlikely option. Toron's analysis ruled out each of these possibilities in turn.

Since he was reluctant to believe the D&M Pyramid might be artificial, he concluded only that "no known mechanism of natural formation could yield a satisfactory account of the observed general characteristics of the object."[7]

Toron went on to create a geometrical model of the D&M Pyramid to investigate its character and properties before the hypothetical damage occurred. His model turned out to be unique, a mathematically rich figure that incorporates acceptable values for the square roots of 2, 3, 5, and *pi*, and the Golden Section ratio of 1:1.618.

While impressive to mathematicians, who realize at once how unlikely it is for such values to arise accidentally, these discoveries have a tendency to confuse the layperson. But it is worth pointing out that they are the first hint of something very strange within a context that is already strange indeed.

The values of the square roots of 2, 3, and 5 are generated by a geometrical figure commonly known as the *vesica piscis*, which was widely used as a religious symbol in ancient times. The Golden Section is known to every student of art, since the use of the ratio in composition produces pictures that are inherently pleasing to the human eye.

---

[7] Quoted from *The McDaniel Report*.

10

PERHAPS THE BEST known lecturer and writer on the Martian anomalies is Richard C. Hoagland, whose interest runs so deep that he founded the Mars Mission, an independent space research and policy group operating just outside New York City. In 1993, he became the winner of the Angström Foundation's First International Angström Medal for Excellence in Science for his work on hyperdimensional physics and its technological implications.

In the course of a continuing investigation, Hoagland made extensive measurements of *all* the curious structures in the Cydonia region and discovered evidence that much of the complex was laid out in accordance with the principles of sacred geometry.

Sacred geometry is the name scholars use for a complex tradition of relationships that influenced the temple architecture of Ancient Egypt and Ancient Greece. The "Face on Mars" is approximately 1.5 miles long by 1.2 miles wide and 0.25 mile high. Eight miles to the southwest, the D&M Pyramid is 1.6 miles long by 1 mile wide by 0.31 mile high.

If these structures are artificial, they make the pyramids of Egypt look like Lego toys.

2 | LIFE, BUT NOT AS WE KNOW IT?

MARS IS THE fourth planet from the Sun. At 24 hours and 37 minutes, its day is much the same as ours. It has a tilted axis of rotation, an atmosphere and seasons, but there the similarities to our own world come to a grinding halt.

The Martian year—which lasts 687 Earth days—is almost double what we're used to. The Martian temperature is chill. At sea level (if there were any seas, which there aren't) the mean is around $-23°$ C. As you stood shivering on the barren surface, you would notice a profound difference in the gravity as well. This planet has a diameter of 6,790 kilometers (4,284 miles), about half that of the Earth, and its density is lower too so that you weigh approximately one third what you would on Earth. The atmosphere is thin and composed predominantly of carbon dioxide, with some nitrogen and argon.

Traces of water have been detected, but not much. What there is seems to be locked into the polar ice caps. But even these aren't composed totally of water ice. Much of them is actually frozen carbon dioxide.

There's a dramatic difference between the planet's hemispheres. Images returned by NASA probes show the southern hemisphere to be old and cratered, very like the surface of our moon. The north, by contrast, seems to be covered in much younger material, perhaps volcanic, perhaps blown there by persistent—and often violent—Martian winds. There are far fewer craters to be seen and the landscape is one of wide, smooth plains. Why there should be such a difference between the two hemispheres is something of a mystery.

Many of the surface features of the planet are huge by Earth standards. The Martian mountain, Olympus Mons, is the largest known volcano in the solar system. It has a diameter of 550 kilometers (347 miles) and a height of roughly 27 kilometers (17 miles). There is a gigantic rift valley near the Martian equator that is 4,000 kilometers (2,524 miles) long. To the south there is a single crater 1,600 kilometers (1,010 miles) in diameter.

To terrestrial eyes, the vista presented by the Martian surface is alien in the extreme. Huge wind-formed sand dunes are common. An immense dune field surrounds the north polar cap. Distorted, flame-shaped landforms composed of wind-blown debris have built up in the lee of many prominences. There are two moons in the sky, both moving fast and one moving very fast indeed.

Knowledge of the interior of Mars is limited, but what evidence we have suggests its structure and chemical content must be very different from that of Earth or the moon. It may have a lower iron-nickel content.

The chemical nature of the Martian soil is unlike terrestrial or lunar rock. If anything, it is something like a heavily weathered clay with naturally occurring radioactive isotopes of potassium, uranium, and thorium.

None of this sounds very promising when it comes to estimating the probabilities of Martian life. Nonetheless, the possibility of life cannot be wholly ruled out.

The ecosphere of a star, as defined by scientists, is the range of distances in which any planets might have water in liquid form, an atmosphere that didn't boil off into space and enough warmth for life to survive.

The ecosphere of our sun includes the planet Mars.

2

AS LONG AGO as 1844, the French astronomer E. L. Trouvelot observed seasonal brightness changes on the surface of Mars. He concluded they were due to vegetation. Others have since confirmed his observations, if not his interpretation. There is a noticeable increase in contrast between bright and dark areas of Mars each spring. Some astronomers have reported they can see color changes as well.

3

GIOVANNI VIRGINIO SCHIAPARELLI was just nine years old when Trouvelot first published his speculations about vegetable life on Mars. They may even have influenced Schiaparelli's choice of career. In 1854, he went to Berlin to study astronomy, and two years later was appointed Assistant Observer at the Pulkovo Observatory in Russia. By 1860 Schiaparelli had joined the staff of the Brera Observatory in Milan. He became its director in 1862.

As an astronomer, Schiaparelli had a distinguished career. He discovered the asteroid Hesperia. He demonstrated that meteor swarms have orbits similar to those of comets. He was among the very first astronomers to observe double stars.

While looking at Mars in 1877 he made the observation for which he became world famous. Through the Brera telescope, Schiaparelli noticed a series of thin, dead straight lines crossing the brighter areas of the Martian surface. Systematic observation of the lines showed they extended hundreds, sometimes thousands, of miles. They also changed with the seasons, exactly like the bright and dark areas observed by Trouvelot. When Schiaparelli published his findings, he speculated that the lines were most likely to be channels on the Martian surface. But he published in Italian, and when his papers were translated into English, the word for channels (*canali*) was inaccurately rendered as "canals." This mistake led to the idea that the "canals" might have been dug by intelligent beings.

L,

AMONG THOSE CAUGHT up in the conjecture was an American astronomer, Percival Lowell. As a member of a distinguished Massachusetts family, Lowell had a considerable personal fortune which he promptly devoted to a study of Mars. During the 1980s, he built a private observatory at Flagstaff, Arizona and trained his telescope on the Red Planet. Like many others, he was able to see Schiaparelli's "canals"; Lowell took the term literally. He was a man with a romantic, even mystical, turn of mind. (One of his books was entitled *Occult Japan*.) He theorized that the faint lines were bands of cultivated vegetation. He believed intelligent inhabitants of the dying world had constructed a planetwide irrigation system, tapping water from the polar ice caps which melted annually.

But Lowell's ideas failed to stand the test of time. There has been scientific controversy not only about his theory, but about the reality of the lines themselves. At one time, it was fashionable to dismiss them as an optical illusion. But when the US spacecraft *Mariner IV* made a close approach to Mars in July 1965, the pictures it sent back made two things clear.

The first was that neither the "canals" nor Lowell's theory about vegetation held water. The second was that immense straight-line formations really do exist on Mars. Scientists variously explain them as mountains, chains of craters, contour boundaries, fault lines, or ridges.

5

ON JULY 20, 1976, the *Viking I* spacecraft that had been photographing the Martian surface launched a robot landing craft that touched down at 22° North latitude, 48° West longitude in the region of Chryse Planitia. A little over a month later, a second probe landed, launched this time from *Viking II*. The site was Utopia Planitia, which lies at 48° North latitude, 226° West longitude.

The landers looked like mechanical insects. Each contained a miniature laboratory equipped to carry out experiments designed to detect the presence (or remains) of organic material. Far from Cydonia, these little craft began to analyze atmosphere and soil samples. Instruments took temperature and wind-speed readings. Cameras rotated to take both visible light and infrared photographs of the immediate environment.

All this activity was aimed at answering three questions:

- Was there any organic material on the Martian surface?
- Were there any objects on the surface that suggested living or even fossilized organisms?
- Was there any indication of bacteria or plant life in the Martian soil?

The first experiment involved direct, sensitive chemical analysis and showed no trace of any organic material on the Martian surface. The results were clear-cut. The second experiment had equally clear-cut results. The cameras gave no indication of any fossil, artifact, or life form in the immediate area.

The third experiment was more complicated. First, the probes heated soil samples in the hope of discovering signs of photosynthesis that would indicate the presence of plants, or chemosynthesis that would indicate the presence of organic compounds. Next, they measured gases released from soil samples exposed to a humid atmosphere or washed in a solution of organic nutrients. Finally, they looked for any release of radioactive gas in soil samples exposed to radioactive organic nutrients.

All three approaches produced positive results. One set of results would have been accepted as incontrovertible proof of biological action had the experiment been carried out on Earth. The scientists in charge of the project decided no life signs were present.

This view was not widely challenged. The only real controversy centered on the fact that the experiments were carried out at just two sites and might be considered too limited in their scope.

6

IN 1980, an interesting, but little publicized, experiment was carried out at the Space Biology Laboratory of Moscow University. Russian scientists created a simulated Martian environment based on the data returned by the *Viking* landers. They then introduced a variety of terrestrial life forms.

Predictably, birds and mammals died within seconds, but reptiles survived for hours and some insects were still alive after weeks. But the real surprise was plant life. Fungi, algae, lichens, mosses, and even beans and cereals like oats and rye not only survived, but, after a period of adaptation, actually thrived.

7

IN 1987, NASA released photographs of Martian "meteorites" found in the Antarctic. One of them was very strange. It looked for all the world as if four stone blocks had been shaped by a mason and joined together. It seemed to be a section of a wall.

8

AUGUST 6, 1996 marked the world premier of *Independence Day*, a Hollywood blockbuster about an alien invasion of Earth. As audiences filed into the movie theater, news broke that NASA scientists had discovered evidence of life on Mars.

But not current life. The breaking story concerned a meteorite (ALH 84001) that crashed into the Allen Hills area of Antarctica 12–13,000 years ago. It was discovered by scientists in 1984. First analysis by NASA, the Open University and the Natural History Museum, London, indicated that the rock contained glass bubbles trapping gases of the same composition as the Martian atmosphere. This led to the conclusion that the meteorite had "splashed off" the Martian surface under the force of an impact. Further analysis hit an even bigger jackpot. Inside the meteorite were chalky structures that contained the fossil signatures of very primitive microscopic life forms.[1] Although it landed on Earth around the end of the last Ice Age, the Martian rock is estimated to be 4.5 *billion*[2] years old—much older than

---

[1] At least according to NASA. Within weeks, scientists at the University of New Mexico, had announced the only life signatures they could find in the rock were complex carbon molecules. In December 1997, another group claimed the "fossils" were just little freaks of geology. A month later, scientists from the Scripps Institute of Oceanography, decided the fossils were organic traces after all, but had resulted from terrestrial contamination. Throughout it all, NASA stuck to its guns.

[2] The American billion is used here and throughout, defined as 1,000 million.

any meteorite previously discovered. Experts think it was part of the original crust when the planet was first formed.

Mars is a cold, dry, barren place today, but work by Dr. Monica Grady of London's Natural History Museum, indicates this was not always so. At the time the fossil bacteria were alive, the Martian climate was hot and wet, consequently much more conducive to the evolution of life.

But NASA administrator Daniel Goldin stressed that when scientists spoke of life on Mars they were not talking about "little green men." When Dr. Doug Milliard of the National Science Museum, London, was asked if the finds suggested there might have been more advanced life on Mars at one time, he quickly denied any direct correlation.

Nobody thought to ask either of them about the "Face."

ๆ

THE OLDEST FOSSILS found on Earth are 3.46 billion years old, discovered in a layer of chert from Western Australia. They are the remains of microscopic bacteria quite similar to those that left their signature on the Martian rock. But the Martian life forms have been dated to 3.6 billion years old, more than 100 million years earlier than their Earth counterparts. This suggests the evolution of life on Mars may have had a 100-million-year head start on the evolution of life on Earth.

Let's assume the pace of evolution on both planets was roughly similar. If so, then intelligence could have appeared on Mars 100 million years earlier than it did on Earth. Likewise, civilization could have appeared on Mars 100 million years earlier than it did on Earth. Our present level of technology could have been reached by Martians 100 million years ago. In the days when dinosaurs roamed the Earth, the Martians could have been planning space flights.

10

IF YOU LEAVE OUT nature, only Martians or creatures from beyond the solar system could have made the "Face on Mars." Scientists don't accept the latter possibility.

11

SETI IS AN ACRONYM for Search for Extraterrestrial Intelligence, a project set up in the late 1980s with the aid of a $100 million NASA grant and now privately funded. Its president, Professor Frank Drake, fully expects to witness the discovery of radio signals from an extraterrestrial civilization before the year 2000. Drake also claims 99.9 percent of his scientific colleagues agree wholeheartedly that intelligent life forms exist outside of Earth. There may even be large populations of them throughout the Milky Way galaxy and beyond.

The root of this conviction is statistical. There are so many galaxies in the known universe, so many stars in each galaxy, that the odds in favor of intelligent life-bearing planets approach certainty.

When Drake founded the first SETI effort, Project Ozma, at the National Radio Astronomy Observatory in Green Bank, West Virginia in 1959, he developed the formula $N = R_* \times f_p \times n_e \times f_l \times f_i \times f_c \times L$ to help calculate the number of detectable civilizations in space.

Although the values allocated to the various factors in this equation have changed over the years, the most *pessimistic* solution suggests there are 1,000 advanced technical civilizations in the Milky Way galaxy alone.

More optimistic values set the figure as high as 100 million.

12

IN 1968 a Swiss author, Erich Von Daniken, suggested that not only is advanced intelligence out there, but it has already visited Earth. Von Daniken's theory was that religious myths of "the gods" actually referred to extraterrestrial visitors and their "miraculous" powers were due to advanced technology.

It was an idea that gripped the mass imagination. Von Daniken's books sold in excess of 25 million copies worldwide. But his theories cut no ice at all with the scientific community. He was accused of misinterpreting, exaggerating and, finally, faking his evidence. What began as an interesting thesis eventually collapsed under the weight of criticism.

13

SCIENTISTS REMAIN SKEPTICAL about visitors from space. They argue that the distances between the stars are just too large to make interstellar travel feasible. Such distances are measured in light-years, each light-year representing some 5,865,696,000,000 miles.

The nearest star in our galaxy is Alpha Centauri, which is 4.3 light-years from Earth. Astronomers have no reason to believe this star system is inhabited. In 1996, they did discover a planet theoretically capable of supporting life. It orbits 70 Virginis, which is 50 light-years away.

In 1961, the Nobel prize-winning US physicist Edward Purcell wrote a special report for the Atomic Energy Commission in which he worked out the energy requirements of relativistic rockets—craft that could travel at a worthwhile fraction of the speed of light. The figure was so enormous he concluded no civilization, however advanced, could possibly take to interstellar travel. The idea, he said, belonged on the back of cereal boxes.

If it's too far for star travelers to visit Earth, it's too far for them to visit Mars. Which means the "Face" was made by Martians.

14

BUT THE "FACE" looks definitely *human*.

The chances against two identical species evolving simultaneously on neighboring planets are 10 to the power of 16,557,000—a figure so immense that it would add a further 1,000 pages to this book to write it out in full.

In order to become familiar with a human face, Martians must once have visited the Earth. A convoluted trail of evidence suggests they may even have founded the human race.

3 | ANCESTRAL CONTACT

ACCORDING TO CURRENT thinking, the ancestors of modern humanity, known as hominids, diverged from apes somewhere between 5 and 8 million years ago.

Hominid remains have been found only in Africa. The scientific consensus accepts these creatures were adapted to life in a tropical climate. They were not human. They were primitive ape-like animals who would, in the course of evolutionary time, eventually *become* human. Their anatomy was different to that of modern man, so paleontologists have few problems sorting out one group of fossils from the other. But they were like humans in one respect. Their upright posture left their hands free for carrying things, manipulating things and, eventually, for making tools.

Tool-making represented an evolutionary watershed for hominids. Many experts believe it was the creation and use of tools that ultimately divided man from the lower animals. The oldest datable tools are chipped pebbles, found at Hadar in Ethiopia. They are 2.5 million years old.

2

EXPERTS HAVE NAMED the early tool-making proto-humans *Homo habilis*. The term translates as "handy man." Their fossil bones were first discovered in 1964 at Olduvai Gorge in Tanzania, East Africa, by the British anthropologist Louis Leakey.

The exact position of *Homo habilis* in human evolution isn't known for sure. Some scientists believe it was the earliest member of our species. Others think it represents an evolutionary transition between an earlier ape-like creature, *Australopithecus africanus*, and later members of the species *Homo erectus*, or "upright man."

Some 1.8 million years ago, members of the species *Homo habilis* were already building their own shelters—traces of them remain in the Olduvai Gorge. They must also have learned to make clothes. Shelter, clothing, tools, and a gradually increasing brain size were the factors that permitted our ancestors to move out of Africa. The first two of these were particularly important since the world was cooling as it moved toward a full-scale Ice Age 1.5 million years ago.

By 1.7 million BPE[1] man was in Asia and using fire. Some time prior to 700,000 BP he moved into Europe. There are traces of early occupation in France, Czechoslovakia, and Yugoslavia. After 700,000 BPE his range widened, but the earlier sites cluster around the Mediterranean basin. Around 120,000 years ago the Neanderthals appeared in western Eurasia. They may not have been truly human, but they were certainly "kissing cousins" to our race. They buried their dead with flowers, engaged in ritual behavior, and seem to have believed in reincarnation.

3

THE FIRST EMERGENCE of modern humanity, *Homo sapiens sapiens*, occurred around 100,000 years ago in southern Africa. These early humans spread throughout Africa, and appeared in Europe some 35,000 years ago. One theory has it they drove the

---

[1] Before the present era.

Neanderthals to extinction. They lived a hunter-gatherer existence until the agricultural revolution caught up with them.

The archaeological consensus links the agricultural revolution with the ending of the last Ice Age, somewhere around 8000 BC. Ice ages do a great deal more than send glaciers flowing south. As the ice sheets advance, they lock up more and more of the world's water, reducing atmospheric moisture and consequently rainfall. The effect in the tropics is a spread of deserts while everywhere sea levels fall and continental outlines change. During the last Ice Age, for example, the British Isles were joined to continental Europe. Once the ice sheets retreat, rainfall increases, and tundra and desert are reclaimed by forest and grassland. Game animals multiply and conditions generally become more suited to the development of farming.

Archaeologists date the emergence of farming to around 8000 BC, in the so-called Fertile Crescent of the Near East (essentially a swath from the Persian Gulf around the northern edge of the Syrian Desert to Palestine and the borders of Egypt). Elsewhere, agriculture appeared around 6000 BC in China and, coincidentally, Mesoamerica.

It was the development of agriculture that led to civilization. By 4000 BC farming had become a way of life throughout most of the Old World. The first urban communities were in place. Civilization was on the march.

This is the consensus. Modern man began in Africa, spread outward into Asia as a primitive hunter-gatherer, started farming at the end of the Ice Age and began building cities a few thousand years later.

You'll notice that nowhere is there any mention of humanity coming down from Mars.

↳

JUST BECAUSE SCIENTISTS have reached a consensus doesn't necessarily mean they've reached the truth.

Consensus science places the entire history of modern humanity in the Pleistocene and Holocene periods, roughly 2 million years ago to the present day. All that human activity is charted by means of fossil bones and a smallish number of artifacts. The most important artifacts are purposely modified animal bones—incised, broken, carved, or scraped—and interesting little items called eoliths, paleoliths, and neoliths.

Eoliths ("dawn stones") are chipped pebbles with one or more edges intentionally worked or worn by use. They are thought to be the earliest known tools. Paleoliths ("old stones") are a little more sophisticated. They are stones purposely chipped into a recognizable tool type. Neoliths ("new stones") are the most advanced stone tools and utensils.

The earliest anatomically modern human fossils recognized by the scientific consensus are dated to about 100,000 years ago and confined to Africa. Even the earliest recognizable proto-humans such as *Homo habilis* and *Homo erectus* are held to have appeared no earlier than the Pliocene, 5 million years ago.

But the idea that there were no anatomically modern humans prior to 100,000 years ago is contradicted by numerous finds. Oddly, they are not confined to Africa.

5

A HUMAN SKULL fragment unearthed at Vértesszöllös, Hungary, was dated between 250,000 and 450,000 years ago. A human footprint with accompanying paleoliths, bone tools, hearths, and shelters, discovered at Terra Amata, France, was dated 300,000 to

400,000 years ago. These suggest modern humanity was in Europe more than 100,000 years before it was supposed to have left Africa.

The evidence is well supported by other finds. They include paleoliths at Torralba in Spain, a partial human skeleton at Clichy and a human jaw and paleoliths at Moulin Quignon, both in France; and two English finds of skeletons, one with associated paleoliths, at Ipswich and Galley Hill near London. All are at least 300,000 years old.

The Ipswich skeleton may be as much as 600,000 years old.

6

THERE IS CONTROVERSY surrounding these discoveries as there is controversy surrounding any discovery that contradicts the consensus view. The Clichy find has been called a hoax, the Moulin Quignon finds forgeries. While the skeleton at Galley Hill is widely believed to be genuine, experts insist it must have been a recent burial in ancient strata.

Only the towering reputation of Louis Leakey, whose African discoveries have made a unique contribution to our understanding of human evolution, protected him from accusations of forgery or hoax when he reported finds of human skull fragments and paleoliths at Kanjera in Kenya, and advanced paleoliths, of modern human manufacture, in the Olduvai Gorge in Tanzania. The latter were dated at 400,000 years ago and the former somewhere between 400,000 and 700,000 years ago. The clear implications of these finds have, however, been generally ignored.

So have the implications of paleoliths, bone tools, incised bone, and *sawn* wood discovered at Cromer Forest Bed in England. Here again the dating is no more recent than 400,000 years ago and may possibly be up to *four times* older.

In Gehe, China, neoliths of a type that indicate full human capacity have been dated to 600,000 years ago. There are hearths, charcoal, human femurs and broken animal bones, all denoting modern humanity, at Trinil in Java. Their date is 830,000 years BPE.

7

SCIENTIST WHO HOLD to the consensus opinion argue that these various artifacts and fossils *cannot* denote anatomically modern human habitation, thus *must be* misdated. Alternatively, they *must be* the remains not of *Homo sapiens* but of the older *Homo erectus*. This logic is based on a double standard. If the evidence supports the consensus, it is readily accepted. If it doesn't, it is routinely—sometimes shrilly—challenged.

Cracks in the consensus case widen when you come to evidence of modern humanity prior to 1 million years ago. The date is critical to the consensus view since it marks the emigration from Africa of the first hominid, *Homo erectus*. This means that any bone fragments or artifacts found outside Africa and dated prior to 1 million years ago can no longer be attributed to *Homo erectus*.

Such finds exist. An anatomically modern human skull discovered in Buenos Aires, Argentina, is dated between 1 million and 1.5 million years ago. A human tooth at Trinil in Java has yielded a date between 1 and 1.9 million years ago. Eoliths at Monte Hermoso, also in Argentina, are believed to be between 1 and 2.5 million years old.

All are borderline cases. If you take the most recent possible dating in each, they might just possibly squeeze into the *Homo erectus* time period—although each find is not typical of *erectus* but of *Homo sapiens sapiens*, modern humanity.

But once you consider finds whose most recent dating lies beyond the magical 1-million-years-ago marker, it's difficult to cling to the consensus case.

8

EOLITHS AND INCISED bones found at St. Prest in France have a recent dating of 1.2 million years, 200,000 years before *Homo erectus* is supposed to have left Africa. There is a possibility they are as old as 2 million years BPE.

Incised bones, dating between 1.2 and 2.5 million years BPE have been found at Val d'Arno in Italy. Eoliths discovered at Ulalinkla, in Siberia, are between 1.5 and 2.5 million years old. There are paleoliths from Yuanmou in China that have yielded an astounding date of 1.7 million years old. Even this figure has been superseded by finds of paleoliths, cut and charred bones, found at Xihoudu in China and eoliths from Diring Yurlakh in Siberia. In both instances they are dated to 1.8 million years BPE.

If anatomically modern humanity existed outside of Africa at such an early date, you might expect evidence for the existence of modern humanity inside Africa at the same time. Such evidence has appeared in the form of a human jaw and eoliths found by Louis Leakey at Kanam in Kenya, and dated between 1.7 and 2 million years BPE.

Further finds by Louis and Mary Leakey at Olduvai, Tanzania, have the same dating. They include polished bones, eoliths, paleoliths, bolas (a type of ball denoting a fairly advanced form of stone work), a stone circle believed to have formed the base of a shelter, and a leather working tool made from bone. The consensus relegates all these finds to the ape-like *Homo habilis*.

Leatherwork, bolas, and shelter have always been held to be well beyond the capacity of *Homo habilis*.

9

HOMO HABILIS IS accepted by the consensus as the earliest of all toolmakers. *Homo habilis* fossils, dating back just over 2 million years, are strictly confined to Africa. Any signs of humanity prior to this date could not possibly be attributed to *Homo habilis* without a serious revision of consensus opinion. An abundance of such signs actually exist . . . and are ignored.

In Nampa, Idaho, a clay figurine was unearthed in 1912 from strata denoting an age of 2 million years BPE. If this was made by *Homo habilis*, "handy man" was a great deal handier in America (where he was not supposed to have existed at all) than in Africa. Eoliths, also dated to 2 million years BPE, indicate that something far more advanced than *Homo habilis* was also wandering the Soan Valley in Pakistan at about the same time.

These are not isolated discoveries. Although disputed or ignored by consensus scientists, the finds continue to multiply. They include eoliths in India; paleoliths in England, Belgium, Italy, and Argentina; flint blades in Italy; hearths in Argentina (and other indications of human-made fire in England); a carved shell, pierced teeth, a pierced bone, and even two human jaws . . . all discovered outside Africa, all bearing a *minimum* date of 2 million years BPE. Some of them may actually be as old as 4 million years BPE.

10

THAT LATTER DATE is doubly unpalatable to the consensus since it would push humanity right out of the Pleistocene into the Pliocene, a whole earlier age. There *is* consensus admission that some very basic stone tools existed in the late Pliocene, but nothing older than 3 million years BPE and definitely only in

Africa where, it is presumed, they were made by the very brightest and best of our most distant and primitive proto-human ancestors.

Here again we have a dividing line cracking under the weight of accumulated evidence. Bone tools, a sawed bone, eoliths and even one neolith found in England, all indicate that late Pliocene tools are *not* after all confined to Africa and are not after all primitive in their construction. These finds have a minimum dating of 2.5 million years BPE.[2]

Available evidence shows that whatever the consensus may claim, there were anatomically modern humans living both inside and outside of Africa right back to the early Pliocene. Their bones, vertebra, and in six cases partial or complete skeletons, have been found in Italy, Argentina, and Kenya. Their toe prints have been found in Belgium, their footprints in Kenya. They have left hearths in Argentina, cut shells, incised bones and paleoliths in Antwerp, Belgium. *Minimum* datings range from 3 million to 4 million years BPE. Maximum dating (for the Antwerp finds) could be as high as 7 million years BPE, which would push them beyond even the Pliocene by some 2 million years.

In other words, the maximum dating of these finds would place humanity in the distant Miocene.

11

THE MIOCENE, an almost unimaginably ancient geological period, began some 25 million years ago. Consensus science says no human beings walked our planet then.

This conclusion is only possible by denying the evidence of a human skull, a partial human skeleton, and a

---

[2] Their possible maximum dating (144 million years BPE) is so ancient I hesitated to introduce it into the main text.

collection of neoliths discovered in four different sites in California. All have been dated in excess of 5 million years. A human skeleton discovered at Midi in France, paleoliths found in Portugal, Burma, and Argentina, a carved bone and flint flakes from Turkey, all have a minimum age of 5 million years, with their maxima varying between 12 and 25 million years.

Paleoliths found at Aurillac in France have been dated between 7 and 9 million years BPE. Human bones from Placer County, California, are known to be older than 8.7 million years. There is an eolith from India, various neoliths, a stone bead, human jaw and skull fragments, spearheads, ladles, and a bow handle—all Californian—that have a minimum dating of 9 million years BPE.

Broken or incised bones from France, Argentina, and Kenya are no less than 12 million years old, as are some Argentinean paleoliths. California and France have respectively provided neolith and paleolith finds dating all the way back to the early Miocene. The paleoliths are at least 20 million years old. Interestingly, the more advanced neoliths are even older, somewhere in excess of 23 million years.

The curiosity of more sophisticated tools at an earlier age begins to form a pattern as you push back even further. Three different finds of paleoliths from Belgium have a minimum dating of 26 million years ago, placing them firmly in an even earlier geological time period, the Oligocene.

A human skeleton, anatomically identical to *Homo sapiens sapiens*, discovered at Table Mountain, California, is at least 33 million years old, as are neoliths and a carved stone from the same site. Here again, the older artifacts are the more highly developed. It's almost as if human skills peaked at some time in the very distant past and then gradually degenerated.

12

CONSENSUS-BREAKING FINDS continue to appear. A human skeleton has been found in Switzerland dating from the remote Eocene, its age estimated between 38 and 45 million years. Eoliths, paleoliths, and a carved stone from England share the same minimum dating, although their maximum age could be older by as much as 10 million years. France has yielded up eoliths, paleoliths, cut wood and even a chalk ball, the *minimum* ages of which range from 45 to 50 million years.

Clearly, the humans who left these various remains could not have evolved in Africa 100,000 years ago. But it requires a massive leap of faith to conclude they evolved on Mars.

4 | SIGNS OF VISITORS

SCIENTISTS DIVIDE THE prehistory of our planet into three eras: the Paleozoic ("ancient life"), the Mesozoic ("middle life"), and the Cenozoic ("recent life"). Each is subdivided into geological time periods, sixteen in total.

The Paleozoic (600 to 250 million years BPE) is divided into six periods: Cambrian (590 million years BPE), Ordovician (505 million years BPE), Silurian (438 million years BPE), Devonian (408 million years BPE), Carboniferous (360 million years BPE), and Permian (286 million years BPE).

The Mesozoic (250 to 65 million years BPE) comprises the three great periods of the dinosaurs: Triassic (245 to 208 million years BPE), Jurassic (208 to 144 million years BPE), and Cretaceous (144 to 65 million years BPE). The dinosaurs vanished from our planet at the very end of the Mesozoic.

The Cenozoic (65 million years BPE to the present), is divided into seven periods: Paleocene (65 million years BPE), Eocene (55 million years BPE), Oligocene (38 million years BPE), Miocene (25 million years BPE), Pliocene (5 million years BPE), Pleistocene (2 million years BPE), and Holocene, that began a mere 10,000 years ago with the ending of the last Ice Age.

If Martians were 100 million years ahead of humans in evolution, they could have turned their minds to space flight sometime during Earth's Cretaceous period.

2

SPACE FLIGHT COULD have been a lot easier for Martians than it has been for humans.

Mars has a mass of just over one tenth that of Earth.
Its surface gravity at the equator is just 3.72 cm per
second squared, as opposed to 9.78 on Earth. Escape
velocity—the speed needed to leave a planet—is 11.2
km per second on Earth. It's only 5 km per second on
Mars. A lower escape velocity means less fuel and a less
efficient engine will get you into space.

Psychologists claim our natural satellite—the
moon—contributed to humanity's interest in space
flight. In lay terms, we looked up, saw it, and wondered
how to get there. Mars has two moons, Phobos and
Diemos, both visible from its surface. They are much
closer to Mars than our moon is to Earth. Our moon
orbits some 384,400 kilometers away. Diemos is only
23,460 kilometers from Mars. Phobos is even closer—a
mere 9,380 kilometers.

The first logical step in any space program is to
reach the nearest astronomical body. Our nearest astronomical body is the moon, which we reached in July
1969. Compared with that trip, reaching Phobos would
have been a piece of cake for the ancient Martians.

Once you reach your satellite, you naturally turn
your attention to your planetary neighbors. Mars has
two—Earth and Jupiter. At its closest approach, Earth
is less than 56 million kilometers from Mars. The closest
Jupiter ever gets is more than 491 million kilometers.
Besides which, what sane Martians would want to land
on Jupiter? They would be crushed by a gravity more
than 600 times what they were used to at home. They
would need almost eleven times the escape velocity to
get off again. And they would be sinking through a
planet that has no real solidity at all.

Jupiter is a giant made of gas. If Martians headed anywhere, it would have been to Earth.

3

THE EARLY HUMAN finds listed in Chapter 3 might be interpreted as showing the scientific consensus is just plain wrong. They could mean modern humanity didn't evolve in Africa 100,000 years ago. It appeared far earlier somewhere else.

But humanity couldn't have appeared earlier than 65 million years BPE, the date that marks the death of the dinosaurs. The remains of dinosaurs are found in sedimentary rock strata all the way from the Middle Triassic epoch, 230 million years ago, to the end of the Cretaceous. Although known fossils probably represent less than 0.0001 percent of all the dinosaurs that lived, there are still so many of them nobody can deny saurian life forms ruled this planet during the Mesozoic era.

Dinosaurs continued to flourish until the end of the Cretaceous period. Then they disappeared. You can hunt more recent rock strata until you're blue in the face and you will find not the slightest trace of any dinosaur. Scientists don't know for sure why they died, only that they did—suddenly, around 65 million years BP.

One explanation for the mass extinction is that mountains forming at the end of the Cretaceous period reduced lowland areas where dinosaurs lived and changed the climate. Climatic change meant changes in plant life. Since they couldn't find their favorite foods, dinosaurs starved.

Another theory, currently fashionable, is that an asteroid collided with the Earth throwing up so much dust that the world was plunged into a time of darkness. Without sunlight, the food chain collapsed. This led to a series of extinctions more or less in order of size—the big eaters went down first.

There is mounting evidence for the asteroid idea,

but nothing conclusive. A few dinosaur species survived for a million years after the impact was supposed to have happened.

But the point is not how the dinosaurs became extinct, merely that they did. It was this extinction that created an evolutionary gap the mammals raced to fill.

While there were dinosaurs on Earth, mammals had no chance to develop. It was only after the dinosaurs had gone that this animal group evolved into its present diversity. Since humanity is a mammal species, there is no way it could have evolved on Earth before 65 million years BPE. Any humans turning up before then had to come from somewhere else.

4

In 1938, Professor W. G. Burroughs, head of the Department of Geology at Berea College, Kentucky, reported the discovery of "footprints . . . sunk into the horizontal surface of an outcrop of hard massive grey sandstone on the O. Finnell farm."

There were three pairs of tracks, showing left and right footprints. Each print had five toes and a distinct arch. The toes were spread apart like those of a human used to walking barefoot. The foot curved back like a human foot to what appeared to be a human heel. There was a pair of prints in the series that showed a right and left foot more or less beside each other. The distance between them is just what you'd expect in human footprints.

The find was made at Rockcastle County, Kentucky, but Professor Burroughs claimed that with the cooperation of Dr. C. W. Gilmore, Curator of Vertebrate Paleontology at the Smithsonian, he was able to show creatures like those who made the Kentucky prints had also lived in Pennsylvania and Missouri.

A Smithsonian ethnologist, David L. Bushnell, made the sensible suggestion that the footprints might have been carved by Indians. Microscopic study soon showed this could not have been the case. The footprints were made on what was once a sandy beach. The composition of the sand grains was consistent with footprints in wet sand, not with later rock carving. Photomicrographs and infrared photographs showed no indication of cutting.

In 1960, H. L. Armstrong wrote in the prestigious scientific publication *Nature* about fossil human footprints found in and around the Paluxy River, near Glen Rose in Texas. Dinosaur footprints were found in the same strata.

In 1968, a fossil collector named William J. Meister split open a block of shale near Antelope Spring, Utah, and found a fossilized human *shoe* print. The heel was indented about an eighth of an inch more than the sole and had the characteristic signs of wear that would mark it as a right shoe. There were trilobite fossils in the same stone. Dr. Clarence Coombs of Columbia Union College, Takoma, Maryland, and geologist Maurice Carlisle, University of Colorado at Boulder, confirmed the find was a genuine fossil. Science authors Michael A. Cremo and Richard L. Thompson carried out a computer analysis of the print and found it deviated in no way from the type of print that would be left by a modern shoe.

In 1983, the *Moscow News* reported the discovery of a fossilized human footprint next to the fossil footprint of a three-toed dinosaur in the Turkmen Republic, part of what was then the southwestern USSR.

5

CONSENSUS GEOLOGISTS BELIEVE that all the fossilized prints mentioned above are fakes, misdated, or genuine fossils created by some hitherto unknown amphibian that just happened to walk on two legs and have feet identical to those of modern humans.

But the existence of humanity at impossibly early periods does not rely on the evidence of fossil prints alone. According to a report in *The Geologist* (December 1862), a human skeleton was found 90 feet below the surface in a coal seam at Macoupin County, Illinois. The bones had a coating of a hard, black, glossy matter, but when this was scraped off were white underneath.

All these finds date back beyond the evolutionary watershed of dinosaur extinction—some of them very far beyond indeed. Only the Paluxy River prints are dated to the Cretaceous. The Turkmen print is Jurassic, Meister's shoe print is Triassic, while the Rockcastle County finds date all the way back to the Carboniferous, which makes them more than 286 million years old. The seam in which the skeleton was found dated between 286 and 320 million years BPE.

It looks as if our visitors arrived a little earlier than we expected.

6

AN EVOLVED SPECIES arriving on Earth from Mars many millions of years ago would not have dressed in skins or walked barefoot, except perhaps for pleasure on a sandy beach. They would have worn shoes and they would have used tools far in advance of the flint scrapers and stone ax heads we associate with our so-called primitive ancestors.

If Earth really was visited, then our most ancient finds should show signs of an advanced technology.

7

AN EIGHTEENTH CENTURY report describes how quarrymen working on the Palace of Justice at Aix en Provence, France, found a hoard of mysteries that included stumps of pillars, worked stones, coins, hammer handles, tool fragments, and a mason's board. No exact dating can be made of this find, but it lay under eleven different rock strata, more than forty feet down.

In 1844 the distinguished Scottish physicist, Sir David Brewster, reported the discovery of a metal nail embedded in a sandstone block from the Kingoodie Quarry in northern Britain. The head of the nail was encased in the nine-inch-thick block where it was found, which would rule out the possibility that it was driven in at some recent date. The block itself is dated to the Devonian, more than 360 million years ago.

A length of gold thread has been dated to much the same period. According to *The Times* of 22 June 1844, it was found by workmen embedded in stone at a depth of eight feet close to the River Tweed.

In 1869, James Parsons and his two sons were reported to have discovered a slate wall with several lines of "hieroglyphic writing" carved in bold relief in a coal mine at Hammondville, Ohio. Geologist Albert G. Ingalls remarks: "If man, or even his ape ancestor, or even that ape's early mammalian ancestor existed as far back as the Carboniferous . . . the whole science of geology is so completely wrong that all the geologists will resign their jobs and take up truck driving."

An eight-carat gold chain was found in a piece of coal by Mrs. S. W. Culp of Morrisonville, USA in 1891. The chain was about ten inches long and completely encased in a large lump of coal she was breaking into smaller pieces. The fact that it was found inside the coal suggests a date of manufacture in excess of 260 million years BP.

There have been so many anomalous finds in Carboniferous strata that it's tempting to conclude Martian visitors to Earth had become fairly widespread by that time. In 1897, for example, a carved stone showing multiple faces of an old man was found at a depth of 130 feet in a coal mine near Webster City, Iowa. The dark gray stone was two feet long, one foot wide, and about four inches thick. Its surface was covered in an incised diamond grid pattern with a version of the face in the middle of each one. Two of the faces are looking to the left, all the rest to the right.

An Oklahoma coal mine yielded up an iron cup in 1912. Frank J. Kenwood of Sulphur Springs, Arkansas, was breaking up a massive lump of coal for use in the furnaces of the Municipal Electric Plant in Thomas, Oklahoma, where he worked. Watched by fellow employee Jim Stall, who confirmed his story, an iron pot fell out, leaving the impression of its shape in the middle of the broken coal. Kenwood was so intrigued he set out to trace the origin of the coal and discovered it came from Wilburton Mine in Oklahoma. The coal there is about 312 million years old. There are unconfirmed reports that a barrel-shaped block of silver, decorated with what look like wheat sheaves, was found in this mine in 1928.

In the same year, workers in another Oklahoma mine discovered a block wall on the coal face at a depth of almost two miles. Atlas Almon Mathis described how while working in a shaft mine at Heavener, Oklahoma, he unearthed several "concrete blocks." Each block was a twelve-inch cube, highly polished on the outside, but filled with gravel. The area of the mine in which Mathis was working suffered a cave-in and he was lucky to escape with his life. When he returned to the coal face he found that the cave-in had exposed a portion of wall made from similar blocks to those he found. Another miner struck what seemed to be an extension of the wall between 100 and 150 yards further along.

5 | IN THE MYTHS OF TIME

THERE IS EVIDENCE of ancient microscopic life on Mars. There is evidence of intelligent engineering on Mars. The presence of a human face on Mars suggests Martians must have visited Earth.

According to the current scientific consensus, no Martian could have seen a human face before 100,000 years BPE, the date modern humanity is believed to have evolved in Africa. There is evidence of humans on our planet at a period long before it was remotely possible for mammalian life to have evolved here. This life *cannot* have evolved on Earth. It *must* have evolved elsewhere.[1]

Fossil evidence so far available suggests that life on Mars had an evolutionary head start—measured in millions of years—over life on Earth. This allows the postulate of a technically advanced civilization evolving on Mars millions of years ago.[2] The postulate is supported by the structures of the Cydonia complex, which repre-

---

[1] Either that or we must face the possibility of time travelers from a distant future—a theme explored in my book *Time Travel: A New Perspective* published by Llewellyn, Minnesota, 1997.

[2] It allows the postulate, but the postulate does not depend on it. The pace of Martian evolution may have been far faster than that on Earth. Indeed, this seems to be the case if you allow the validity of the earliest traces of intelligent life on our planet.

sent feats of engineering far more sophisticated than anything our own civilization could yet attempt.[3]

Because of the lower Martian gravity, the slower Martian escape velocity and the nearness of both Martian moons, space travel would have been easier for Martians and may have developed at an earlier stage of the Martian culture than it has in our own.

The nearest planet to Mars is Earth. Indications of "humanity" on Earth at ludicrously early periods such as the Carboniferous may be explained by the theory of visits by technically advanced humanoid aliens from neighboring Mars.

2

YOU MIGHT REASONABLY imagine that the earliest visits by Martians to Earth involved robot probes. These would have been followed up by piloted vessels carrying no more than one or two brave travelers from Mars.

But unlike our own space flights to date, if Martians did come to Earth, they would have landed on a planet already supporting life. The study of this phenomenon would have drawn them like a magnet. Early Earth would contain many clues to the mystery of their own evolution.

It seems likely that as soon as was technically feasible, the Martians would have established a colony of observers on Earth.

---

[3] Richard Hoagland maintains that the D&M Pyramid incorporates information about a multidimensional physics which can be tested against observable phenomena on Earth and throughout the solar system. I have not included his theory in this book since I am unqualified to judge the evidence he presents.

3

THERE WAS, in Arizona, a closed self-contained ecosphere in which plants, animals, and a small number of humans lived in a self-sustaining environment for several years. The project was planned as a prototype for the type of self-sustaining domed colony that might one day be established on another planet.

Domes are not the only possibility. More sophisticated approaches include planetary and genetic engineering. In the first instance, Martians would have changed our atmosphere and ecosphere to allow them to survive unprotected on the Earth's surface. This is perfectly possible for an advanced civilization—there are "think tank" corporations in the United States that have already drawn up plans for terraforming other planets. But one important factor makes this approach unlikely: It would have destroyed the environment the Martians arrived to study.

The second option is more logical. After initial visits in spacesuits or under domes, it would make sense for Martians to breed a subspecies of their own kind (using genetic engineering techniques) capable of breathing Earth's air, utilizing Earth materials, and surviving unsupported on Earth's surface. It might even be that at some stage in the aeons-long colonization program, the Martians conducted a second genetic engineering experiment by manipulating the chromosomes of a primitive, evolving, ape-like creature to create a new humanoid in their own image.

This is a powerful and appealing fantasy, as is its logical corollary that, since Mars is now a desert, some primeval disaster must have overtaken the home planet, marooning the surviving colonists on Earth. They would have worked hard to duplicate the Martian civilization and may even have succeeded for a time. But lack of access to the parent culture, a natural slow degeneration, or possibly some widespread geological catastrophe would eventually have erased all knowledge of humanity's Martian genesis.

4

THERE ARE SEVERAL mythic themes with worldwide distribution. One is the myth of ancient giants. Its most familiar expression is biblical. The Old Testament has numerous references to ancient giants. They begin with Genesis:

> There were giants in the earth in those days; and also after that, when the sons of God came in unto the daughters of men, and they bare children to them, the same became mighty men which were of old, men of renown.[4]

The Book of Numbers describes how the Lord commanded Moses to send men to search the land of Canaan. When the scouting party returned they:

> . . . brought up an evil report of the land which they had searched unto the children of Israel, saying, The land, through which we have gone to search it, is a land that eateth up the inhabitants thereof; and all the people that we saw in it are men of a great stature. And there we saw the giants, the sons of Anak, which come of the giants: and we were in our own sight as grasshoppers, and so we were in their sight.[5]

In Deuteronomy, Moses mentions the Emims "which also were accounted giants" as having lived in the land of the Moabites "in past times."[6]

The land of the Ammonites shared a similar history:

---

[4] Gen. 6:4.
[5] Num. 13:32–33.
[6] Deut. 2:10–11.

"That also was accounted a land of giants: giants
dwelt therein in old time; and the Ammonites call
them Zamzummims; A people great, and many, and
tall, as the Anakims; but the Lord destroyed them
before them; and they succeeded them, and dwelt
in their stead."[7]

In the third chapter of Deuteronomy, Og the King of
Bashan is described as the last remnant of the ancient
giants. He slept on an iron bedstead nine cubits long
and four cubits wide. The term cubit meant different
things in different parts of the ancient world, but here
the term is used by Moses, an initiate of the Egyptian
priesthood, so almost certainly the standard "royal cubit" of just over twenty-five inches would have been
meant. This makes Og's bedstead more than eighteen
feet long and eight feet wide. Bashan itself was called
the "land of giants" at one period.

In Joshua there is twice mention of a "valley of the
giants" (15:8 and 18:16), and again in Joshua (17:15) reference to "the land of the Perizzites and of the giants."
After this period of biblical history giants disappear
from the record.

But the Bible isn't the only source of an ancient tradition of giants. According to the Greek poet Hesiod,
a race of giants (the Titans) appeared as the result of a
union between Earth and Heaven. Greek myths tell of a
struggle between the giants and the gods of Mount
Olympus. The gods won and the giants were wiped out.

There are giants in Norse sagas too. They were primeval beings existing before the gods and were overcome by them exactly as in the Greek myths.

Folklore describes giants as mortals who inhabited
the world in early times. Corineus, the legendary hero
of Cornwall, in England, is supposed to have slain the

---

[7] Deut. 2:20–21.

giant Gogmagog by hurling him from a cliff. But Gogmagog was not believed to have been the only giant inhabiting Cornwall in that distant age—just the greatest of them. Another version of the same story has Brutus, the legendary founder of Britain, capturing two Cornish giants, Gog and Magog.

The ancient giants Druon Antigonus and Gayant are still carried in effigy during annual processions at Antwerp, in Belgium and Douai, in France, respectively. Hill figures such as the Cerne Abbas giant in Dorset, England, commemorate the widespread belief. All ancient giants were human (or at least humanoid) in form.

An ancient European tradition holds that giants were never really a race apart. All people had once been taller and stronger but had degenerated after a Golden Age.

Any evolution of Martian "humanity" took place on a planet that has 38 percent the gravitational pull of Earth. This would lead to giantism.

5

As WIDESPREAD as giant legends is the idea that things were once a good deal better, more advanced, more wonderful than they are today—the myth, in other words, of a prehistoric Golden Age.

In about 700 BC the Greek historian Hesiod wrote of a time when Chronus was king of the gods and humanity lived free from pain, toil, and the effects of aging. Persian texts describe Zoroaster's vision of a four-branched tree which the god Ahura Mazdah interpreted as symbolizing the four prehistoric kingdoms of Iran. The first of these, represented by a golden branch, was established at a time of peace and plenty.

The Romans were so convinced of the reality of a prehistoric Golden Age that Virgil confidently predicted its return about 20 BC. He believed that year would see a world in which crops would grow without toil, war and commerce would disappear, the snake would no longer bite, and honey would run freely from oak trees . . . all indications of the way humanity once lived.

Hindu mythology, adopted by Buddhism, postulates a cyclical history in which four "ages" or *yugas* endlessly repeat over aeons of time. The first age, the *Krita Yuga*, now lost in the mists of Indian prehistory, was a time of righteousness and piety when humanity had a profound understanding of spiritual forces.

Norse myths, outlined in the twelfth century *Völuspá*, describe how chaos was overcome at the moment of the first creation and a wise humanity walked a peaceful earth.

Chinese traditions include fragments of a semi-mythic era in which the Middle Kingdom was ruled by a legendary Yellow Emperor who learned the arts of architecture, acupuncture, and erotic bliss while his subjects enjoyed unprecedented peace and plenty.

These stories *might* reflect distorted memories of a prehistoric civilization grounded in an early Martian colonization. All the same, myths are myths. Nobody goes digging on Mount Olympus for signs of Zeus or Hera. Unless there's some hard evidence to underpin the myths.

6 | PARADISE LOST

THE EARLIEST PRESENTATION of the Golden Age as an historic fact is in the *Dialogues* of Plato, a Greek philosopher who lived between about 428 and 348 BC. Plato quoted Egyptian sources to describe an advanced prehistoric culture which he believed had developed the ideal political system. He located the home of this culture "beyond the Pillars of Hercules," and dated its collapse to about 9600 BC.

This places the heyday of this lost civilization toward the end of the Ice Age, a time when most of us believe the planet was occupied by cave men.

2

WE NOW KNOW cave men didn't live in caves. In the past century, archaeologists have become convinced Pleistocene humanity lived in huts, tents, or rock-shelters. There was some occupation of cave-mouths, but no evidence of permanent habitation of deep caverns.

There *were* some people who moved into caves, but only temporarily. Investigation of a few sites, particularly in the French Pyrenees, has unearthed evidence of hearths and other signs of occupation. They were left by people who came to the caverns for a specific purpose—to create works of art.

When Marcelino Sanz de Sautuola announced his discovery of the first such Ice Age art gallery at Altamira, Spain in 1876, he was denounced as a fraud.

Experts claimed the paintings were far too good to be the product of "ignorant savages." They decided de Sautuola had hired a modern artist to fake them. So vicious were the attacks that they contributed to his early death in 1888. But de Sautuola was right and the experts were wrong. The pictures he discovered *had* been painted by people who lived *c.* 13,550 BC.

It turned out that Ice Age art was not confined to this single site in Spain. There were subsequent discoveries of artworks in Arabia, Australia, Brazil, China, France, India, Japan, Korea, Kwazulu, Mexico, Namibia, North America, Patagonia, Peru, Portugal, Sicily, Zaire, and Zimbabwe. Some may be as old as 40,000 years. Some are definitely as old as 30,000 years. There is even evidence for the use of pigment dating back at least 125,000 years.

The creation of art requires sophistication and sensitivity. It also requires an environment that can support leisure activity. It is difficult to see how such an environment could have existed in the Ice Age. You have to expend more energy to survive in a cold climate than a hot one. In an Ice Age, every waking moment of primitive humanity should have been devoted to the necessities of survival—the search for firewood, shelter, food, and clothing. There should have been no time left over for frivolities like art. Yet not only *was* there time left over, but skeletal remains show no sign of rickets or other indications of malnourishment. Despite harsh conditions, there is little indication of starvation or injury. There is no indication at all of illness. War—even in the form of intertribal conflicts—seems to have been unknown.

What the evidence indicates is a well-fed, fit and healthy people who found no difficulty at all in keeping warm and had sufficient leisure time to express their creativity in painting. All the same, the paintings don't exactly show a city skyline. They depict mainly bison, auroch cattle, fox, mammoth, lion, bear, fish, reptiles, birds, and even insects. Plants are also represented, as are nonfigurative designs which some experts believe may represent patterns seen during trance. In other words, they show the preoccupations of a tribal hunter-gatherer community that was a far cry from any fancy Martian civilization.

3

DESPITE THIS, Plato's account of a prehistoric civilization has stimulated the interest of a great many authors—one estimate puts the total in excess of 2,000, another multiplies this figure by ten. There have been some members of the academic establishment who thought there might be something in it.

In 1909 K. T. Frost advanced what came to be called the Minoan Hypothesis, which related Plato's story to the collapse of Minoan Crete. For Frost there were three areas of similarity between Plato's account and the historical reality of Minoa. Minoan Crete represented an advanced civilization with ancient roots; it was island based and its cultural collapse seemed to have been due to the devastation caused by an immense earthquake. His hypothesis was largely ignored until 1967 when archaeological discoveries by Professor S. Martinatos seemed to give it additional support.

But there was still no question of accepting an Ice Age antiquity for the lost civilization. Professor A. G. Galanopoulos of the Athens Institute of Seismology, put forward the ingenious theory that all the figures quoted in Plato's story had been multiplied by ten. When this was corrected, it not only made sense of his description of a massive capital city but also put the destruction of the culture around 1500 BC, thus placing the cultural collapse at about the time an eruption of the Santorini volcano destroyed Minoan Crete.

Like Frost, Galanopoulos disregarded the fact that Minoan Crete lay inside, not outside, the Pillars of Hercules. Furthermore, in the late 1980s, radiocarbon dating put paid to this ingenious hypothesis by showing that the volcanic eruption supposed to have destroyed Crete occurred *before* the Minoan culture reached its peak, let alone collapsed.

Even today, some scholars insist that Plato's story reflects memories of ancient Crete, possibly because the Galanopoulos theory left intact the orthodox consensus on the development of civilization.

L

IN THE NINETEENTH century anthropologists developed a theory of cultural evolution that divided human progress into three stages: savagery, barbarism, and civilization. At the time, civilization was restricted to ancient Egypt, Assyria, Greece, and Rome. Within the past century, archaeological research has more than doubled this list. The earliest civilization is now believed to be the Sumerian in Mesopotamia, dating *c.* 5000 to 4000 BC. The Minoan and Mycenaean civilizations that preceded classical Greece in the Aegean are dated *c.* 3000 to *c.* 1000 BC. The Indus civilization, which had the largest geographical distribution of all Old World civilizations, peaked from *c.* 2300 to 1700 BC. The Shang civilization of the Hwang Ho Valley in North China emerged in about 1600 BC. The ancient civilizations of the New World (in Mesoamerica and the Andean region of South America) are even more recent—*c.* 1200 BC.

While there is some room to tinker with the dates and a degree of difference between various experts as to what actually constitutes a civilization, the established view remains that prior to 5000 BC all was barbarism and savagery throughout the world.

5

PLATO'S ACCOUNT OF a prehistoric civilization referred to the island of Atlantis, a name now guaranteed to send any reputable scholar diving for cover. Although of immense public interest, Atlantis has become the domain of cranks.[1] It was not always so.

Crantor, an early follower of Plato, accepted the story as history and even claimed to have confirmed it. He did this by interviewing Egyptian priests, who not only validated Plato, but showed him columns of hieroglyphs that gave the complete account.

The geographer Marcellus, who lived in the first century BC, recorded in his *Ethiopic History* the existence of three large and seven small Atlantic islands inhabited by people who retained traditions of Atlantis and its empire. The Stoic philosopher Poseidonios, (c. 135 to c. 51 BC) a mentor of Cicero, went on record with the statement that "it is possible that the story about the island of Atlantis is not a fiction." Neoplatonists like Proclus, the philosopher who succeeded Syrianus as head of the Platonic Academy in Athens, accepted this completely, as did Iamblichus, the fourth century authority on Neoplatonism.

Kosmas, a sixth century Egyptian monk, maintained in his *Christian Topography* that the sinking of Atlantis was no more than a garbled version of the Biblical Flood, but as such had historical validity.

A brief mention of the lost civilization is contained in *De Imagine Mundi*, a work compiled by Honorius of Autun around AD 1100. Thereafter, interest waned for several centuries.

---

[1] A poll of US newspaper people ranked the reemergence of Atlantis the fourth most important story they could imagine ever covering—five points higher than the Second Coming of Jesus Christ.

There was a widespread revival following the discovery of the Americas. Francesco López de Gómara, a Spanish historian, became the first to suggest, in 1553, that Plato had based his story on rumors of the New World. How the rumors had reached him, de Gómara did not explain.

The idea was taken up by Elizabeth I's Court Astrologer, Dr. John Dee (who labeled the Americas "Atlantis" on one of his maps), and later by Francis Bacon.

The speculation continued as late as 1855 when the weight of facts finally killed it.

6

THE SEARCH FOR the "actual" location of Atlantis remains a popular preoccupation. In a straw poll of 200 writers on the subject, seventy-eight had not only decided on the historical reality of Atlantis, but confidently placed it on an Atlantic island. The next most popular location—Crete—had only five supporters. After that, the guesses ranged as far afield as Central America and the North Pole.

Several of the books surveyed were dedicated to readings by America's famous "sleeping prophet" Edgar Cayce who was able to determine psychically a great deal of information about Atlantis and predict (incorrectly) the date on which it would reemerge from the Atlantic seabed.

In the late 1960s, Atlantis was swallowed up by a new fad—Erich Von Daniken's theory that Earth had been visited in the distant past by astronauts. Suddenly these visitors became the founders of Atlantis. The origins of Plato's prehistoric civilization were lifted right off the planet. But not to Mars.

7 | A MYSTERIOUS MAP

AS THE WILDER theories multiplied, it became difficult for any serious scholar to contemplate the possibility of a prehistoric civilization. But one scholar did. His name was Charles Hapgood, an American professor of the history of science.

The sequence of events that was to involve Hapgood in the 1960s actually began in 1929. That was the year an ancient map was discovered in the Topkapi Palace museum in Istanbul, Turkey. The map, dated 919 in the Muslim calendar (i.e., 1513), originally belonged to a Turkish pirate named Piri ('Admiral') Re'is. A copy was deposited in the American Library of Congress while a further copy was presented by a Turkish naval officer to the United States Navy Hydrographic Office.

In 1956, the second copy came to the attention of a professional cartographer named M. I. Walters. He found it an extraordinary document. For an era when maps were largely products of the map-maker's imagination, this one was astonishingly accurate. It showed the Mid-Atlantic Ridge, which you can detect today only by sonar. It showed an accurate outline of South America. It showed the correct longitudes of countries from Morocco to the Ivory Coast in North Africa. It showed Antarctica, a land that was believed to have been undiscovered before 1818.

Walters loaned the map to his friend Alington H. Mallery, a retired navigator who devoted his time to the study of old maps. Mallery discovered that the

Antarctic continent had been mapped before it was covered by ice.

2

IT TRANSPIRED THAT Piri Re'is had not made the map himself, but had copied it from earlier sources. He claimed one was a map made by Columbus, but his remaining *nineteen* sources were all maps rescued from the Library of Alexandria when it was destroyed by Arab invaders in AD 640. The Alexandrian Library, founded by Ptolemy I (*c.* 367 to 283 BC) contained a unique collection of papyri, tablets, and artifacts from the ancient world and was one of the main reasons why Alexandria became the foremost Hellenistic scientific center.

When Professor Hapgood heard of Mallery's findings, he set a student group at Keene State College, New Hampshire, to studying a whole collection of ancient maps, including that of Piri Re'is. What emerged from their study was this:

First, medieval portolans proved in many cases to be just as accurate as modern maps. They sometimes showed features—like the island of Cuba—about which the map-makers should have had no knowledge. An ancient Chinese map, cut in stone around AD 1137, included indications that it had been copied from the same source maps as the portolans. This suggested the European map mystery was worldwide.

Next, the Piri Re'is map itself proved to be a careless combination of the 20 earlier maps. Large stretches of coastline had disappeared and Re'is had shown the River Amazon twice. Hapgood found, however, that if he corrected for an error made by the Greek astronomer Eratosthenes in calculating the size of the Earth, the accuracy of the Piri Re'is map increased substantially.

Next came the way the map was made. Modern maps rely on something called the Mercator projection which lays down geographical features on a grid of latitude and longitude. Ancient maps were drawn from an arbitrary center. The Piri Re'is map followed the ancient custom, but the actual center from which it was drawn lay off the map itself. Calculation showed it had to lie in Egypt, specifically at a spot named Syene, on the River Nile, roughly equivalent to modern Aswan.

3

THE IMPORTANCE OF Syene is that it was used as a special marker in ancient times. On 21 June, the day of the summer solstice, the midday sun was reflected in a well at the site. This curiosity was used by Eratosthenes to calculate the size of the Earth since it indicated that Syene was on a direct line between the Sun and the Earth's center.

Eratosthenes determined that the sun observed at Alexandria (where he was Chief Librarian) was south of the vertical by about 1/50 of a full circle. He calculated that the Earth's circumference would be fifty times the north-south distance between the two localities. This was a good estimate of the size of our planet, but the final figure did contain a margin of error.

The inclusion of the Eratosthenes error and the centering of the map on Syene seemed to Hapgood a clear indication that Piri Re'is had told the truth when he claimed his map had been copied from ancient originals. Those originals must have been Greek.

4

BUT THIS DISCOVERY simply pushed the problem back in time. Nothing in the historical accounts suggests the Ancient Greeks were worldwide sailors. Most of their voyages were confined to the Mediterranean. If they had accurate maps, they were certainly not the result of firsthand observation.

These maps too had to be copied from still earlier sources. The earlier sources had not been corrupted by the Eratosthenes error. They were even more accurate than the Greek versions Piri Re'is had seen. Hapgood's analysis produced evidence that the originals of the Greek maps must themselves have used some form of latitude/longitude projection, exactly like sophisticated modern maps.

All this led him to the conclusion that the distant originals of the Piri Re'is map had been created by a nation of seafarers, unknown to history, who possessed instruments for finding longitude "undreamed of by the Greeks.") Here, for the first time, was proof of a lost civilization.

5

THE INCLUSION OF the Eratosthenes error placed the Greek versions of the Piri Re'is map sometime after the third century BC—the time when Eratosthenes made his calculation. But this was no help in determining the dating of the originals. Hapgood examined other clues. He quickly confirmed Mallery's conclusion that the Antarctic continent had been mapped at a time when it was free of ice. A second map, attributed to Oronteus Finaeus and dated 1531, also showed an ice-free Antarctica and marked the location of the South Pole.

Today, we know the Antarctic outline to be accurate because of the findings of a scientific expedition that took depth soundings in 1949. Hapgood was faced with the choice of an ancient civilization as technically sophisticated as our own, or a civilization that sailed the seas at a time before ice sheets hid the Antarctic coastline. The most recent advance of Antarctic ice was around 4000 BC, which meant the prehistoric civilization must have flourished before that date. Other evidence convinced Hapgood it must have been a very long time before.

Several maps studied showed Scotland and parts of Sweden still glaciated, and suggested the level of the Aegean was much lower than it is today. In other words, these maps seem to have been based on originals made while the Ice Age still held the planet in its frozen grip. But since the ice sheets retreated around 8000 BC, the implication was that the lost civilization flourished before then.

Another Turkish map, that of Hadji Ahmed, drawn in 1550, showed the North Pole and seemed to indicate a land bridge between Alaska and Siberia across the Bering Strait. It is known that such a land bridge did exist, but only before 12,000 BC.

6

IN *CRITIAS*, Plato gives a mythological outline of the origins of *his* lost civilization, telling how the gods divided Earth into allotments in order to establish humanity. His description of the Atlantean continent and its inhabitants is couched in far less mythic terms. It reads like history. Running halfway along the entire length of the island was a fertile coastal plain. Some miles away, in the center of the island, was a low mountain, possibly little more than a hill, on which developed the island's most ancient city. This city was surrounded by three moats, traditionally associated with the god Poseidon. The account contains a lengthy description of abundant forestation, vegetation and animal life, including elephants, which suggests the climate was tropical in nature. There was mining for a now unknown ore, orichalcum, described as "more precious than anything but gold."

The hilltop city became the nation's capital. A canal was cut from the sea to the outermost ring moat making an inland port. The moats themselves were bridged in several places and further smaller canals cut between them, with their entrance and exit points guarded by towers. Walls surrounded each moat. The outer was coated in brass, the middle in tin and the inner in orichalcum. There were public and private baths, artificial fountains, running water—some of it seems to have been drawn from a volcanic hot spring—and even a racetrack. Locally quarried stone, black, red and white, was used for almost all the building work.

Beyond the city, transport and irrigation were provided by a network of canals, so massive that Plato had difficulty in believing the ancient report. Each canal was a uniform 600 feet wide and the network as a whole extended for more than 1,000 miles.

Plato talks of spearmen in the barracks, triremes in the harbors. There is no mention of the internal combustion engine, the computer, the spaceport, or the homeward rocket aimed at Mars.

8 | PHOENIX RISING

MANY BELIEVERS in Atlantis also believe that Atlanteans founded the civilization of Ancient Egypt. Plato disagreed. In his *Timaeus*, he describes a time when a confederation of Atlantean kings gathered an army to invade both Egypt and Greece. The plan was stopped by fighters from the city-state of Athens who not only pushed back the invaders, but also gained freedom for African, Mediterranean, and European territories they already held.

This cameo clearly shows Plato accepted that Egypt was up and running at a time when Atlantean power was at its height. It did not have to wait for its foundation until Atlantis sank.

2

THE PRIESTS OF Sais on the Nile delta told the Greek politician Solon (the source from whom Plato drew his story) that their sacred records showed Egypt was founded 8,000 years previously—a date approaching 9000 BC.

The Egyptian priest Manetho who lived in Ptolemaic Egypt sometime between 347 and 285 BC pushed Egypt's origins back further still. He recorded a predynastic royal line that stretched for 13,777 years. He also claimed an even earlier line of "Horus-kings," predated by a dynasty of demigods. The combined periods of the Horus-kings and demigods stretched back a further 15,150 years. There is not a respected Egyptologist alive today who will accept these datings. Even Manetho's *early* commentators could not stomach them.

∃

THE *TURIN PAPYRUS*, a hemetic manuscript dated *c.* 1400 BC and still considered the most reliable of existing Egyptian king lists, supports Manetho's claim that there were three distinct historical periods prior to the familiar Egypt of dynastic times.

The first of these, the predynastic kings, is given as lasting 13,420 years which is reasonably close to Manetho's figure of 13,777. The second period, that of the Horus-kings, is listed in the *Turin Papyrus* as lasting far longer than Manetho imagined—23,200 years as opposed to Manetho's figure of 15,150 for the *combined* period of the Horus-kings and demigods. The papyrus also recognizes the era of the demigods, but has been damaged so the time period assigned to it is now missing.

The close relationship between Manetho's immediate predynastic timescale and that of the *Turin Papyrus* suggests each was drawn from the same source. Given the vast stretches of time involved, the discrepancies of the remaining figures may not be too surprising.

Depending on which source you consult, the Egyptians placed the foundation of their state somewhere between 9000 BC and a date earlier than 37,000 BC. Modern Egyptologists don't believe it. For them, Egypt achieved unity under King Menes soon after 3100 BC. Its history was then divided into three Kingdoms—Old, Middle, and New—and thirty-one native dynasties. Although prior to 3100 BC, signs of habitation in the Nile Valley stretch back to 18,000 BC, there is no sign whatsoever of an advanced civilization.

4

ACCORDING TO ARCHAEOLOGISTS, by 4000 BC Neolithic villagers had begun to build dikes and a canal network to control the Nile for irrigation. Conventional wisdom has it that as the population grew, a central authority was required because the work involved many communities. This led to the emergence of two kingdoms: Lower Egypt comprising the broad Nile delta north of Memphis, and Upper Egypt which extends southward along the narrow ten- to twenty-mile-wide valley as far as the first cataract at Aswan.[1] Each kingdom contained a number of tribal districts, or nomes, formerly ruled by independent chiefs. Menes, whose tomb was discovered in 1897, was ruler of Upper Egypt. He united the two kingdoms by war and founded the First Pharaonic Dynasty with its capital at Memphis.

This consensus picture suggests a gradual evolutionary process in the Nile Valley with civilization eventually emerging out of progressively sophisticated barbarism. But there are problems with the evidence.

5

ARCHAEOLOGIST MICHAEL HOFFMAN, a project prehistorian in the Hierakonopolis expedition, writes:[2]

Although approximately 15,000 Predynastic graves have been unearthed and great numbers of Pro-

---

[1] The terms Upper and Lower Egypt tend to be confusing to those who consult a modern map, since Lower Egypt appears above (i.e., to the north of) Upper Egypt. The division arose, however, in relation to the flow of the Nile: Upper Egypt is upriver.

[2] In *Egypt Before the Pharaohs,* Ark Books, London, 1980.

todynastic and Archaic burials recovered, there is sadly almost no usable demographic information available . . . We cannot, therefore, compare the relative sizes, life expectancies and patterns of mortality among local late prehistoric and early historic Egyptian populations.

He goes on to mention the "regrettable lack of excavated settlement sites in Upper Egypt" and consequently can offer only "some intelligent guesses" about the types of changes that were occurring in the villages and towns of Egypt at the time of the unification.

One of these guesses is that there was a population shift in late predynastic times. Why it happened is unknown. Among the possibilities are a change of climate, a religious impetus, or both.

It was the concentration of a population, possibly around a ceremonial center, triggered by environmental events, that provided a group of people of sufficient permanence and size for the emerging political elite to organize. Thus population concentration (if not actual growth) played a crucial role in the rise of civilization.[3]

You would not be the first to find this statement woolly.

The civilization of dynastic Egypt gives every appearance of having arisen fully formed on the banks of the Nile. As Hoffman tacitly admits, there is precious little hard evidence of a gradual evolution. The trouble is, there is precious little hard evidence of Egyptian civilization extending back into the Ice Age either. Unless you're prepared to listen to John Anthony West.

---

[3] *Ibid.*

6

JOHN ANTHONY WEST is a tour guide in Egypt. He has maintained for years that the Great Sphinx on the Giza plateau was built around 10,000 BC by survivors of Atlantis. Professional Egyptologists disagree. They insist the Sphinx was created around 2500 BC by the pharaoh Khafre. The face of the Sphinx, they claim, is the face of Khafre. It is possible to test this theory. Khafre was the son of Khufu. The pyramid that bears his name is almost as vast as the Great Pyramid of his father. Khafre's valley temple, linked to his pyramid by a causeway, contained statues of him carved from Nubian diorite, which is an exceptionally hard igneous rock. The statues have withstood the ravages of time so we know exactly what this pharaoh looked like. The question is, did he look like the Sphinx?

Unless you are a professional Egyptologist, this is not a particularly easy question to answer. The Sphinx is far less well preserved than Khafre's statues. It has, for example, lost much of its nose[4] and the remainder of the face is heavily weathered. Nonetheless, most Egyptologists can see a resemblance at once. But Frank Domingo can't. Domingo is a senior forensic scientist with the New York Police Department. He has specialized in matching photofit picture with suspects. In this case the suspect was Khafre (as revealed in his diorite statues) and the "photofit" was the Sphinx. Domingo made measurements both of the Sphinx and the statue of Khafre in Cairo Museum. With the aid of these measurements he constructed profiles of both. Even after you allow for the missing nose, the profiles are completely different.

---

[4] Legend has it as the result of target practice by Napoleon's soldiers, although this is now disputed.

7

SINCE NOBODY LISTENS to an amateur, John Anthony West tried to persuade respected scientists to take his theories seriously. His efforts were hindered by his outspoken views on Atlantis, but he did manage to make friends with some academics. One of them was Professor Robert Eddy, of Boston University.

As a professor of rhetoric, Eddy was in no position to check West's claims directly. But he knew a man who could. He approached Professor Robert Schoch, a permanent faculty member of the Division of Science and Mathematics in the College of General Studies at Boston University. Schoch took his Ph.D. in geology and geophysics at Yale. He was eminently qualified to evaluate the real age of the Sphinx.

Schoch was reluctant to get involved and did so only as a favor to Eddy. When he met West and heard his ideas at firsthand, he was not persuaded. The Sphinx had been examined and reexamined for more than a century. Schoch thought there was little real likelihood that the consensus dating was inaccurate. He did, however, agree to fly to Egypt and see the ancient monument for himself. In 1991 he made the journey and changed his mind about the dating of the Sphinx.

8

ONLY TWO THINGS can weather stone—wind and water. Wind weathers stone by carrying abrasive particles across its surface. Water usually weathers stone in the form of rain which dissolves microscopic layers from its surface. The pattern of weathering in each case is distinctive and completely different.

When Robert Schoch first stood beneath the towering Sphinx, he recognized at once that the weathering pattern it displayed was that of water. Today, Egypt is one of the driest countries in the world. Annual rainfall over Cairo averages no more than an inch a year. By comparison, parts of England have forty times that much. There is simply not enough rain falling on the Sphinx today to create noticeable water weathering. More to the point, there has not been enough rain in Egypt for several thousand years to cause the pattern Schoch saw. The last period of heavy rainfall and flooding in the country was the period of the Nabian Pluvial, which ended around 3000 BC, about 500 years before the Sphinx was supposed to have been built.

Schoch compared the weathering pattern of the Sphinx with that of neighboring Fourth Dynasty tombs. The patterns were different, showing the structures dated from different times.

By the time he completed his examination, Professor Schoch concluded the Sphinx must have been built in stages. The core body, in his opinion, dated to between 7000 and 5000 BC. It wasn't the 10,000 BC John Anthony West had been hoping for, but it was anything between 2500 and 4500 years earlier than the consensus date. It was between 1500 and 3500 years earlier than the supposed foundation of the Egyptian civilization.

9

EGYPTOLOGIST CAROL REDMOUNT of the University of California was quoted in the *Los Angeles Times* as saying Schoch's revised date was impossible. There was neither the will, the governing institutions, nor the technology to create the statue at the date suggested. To claim otherwise flew in the face of everything we knew about Ancient Egypt. Peter Lacovara, assistant curator at the Egyptian Department of the Museum of Fine Arts in Boston, said the revised dating was ridiculous. Egyptologists had the real chronology pretty well worked out. There were no big surprises in store. The Egyptologist Dr. K. Lal Gauri claimed the evidence of weathering was irrelevant when it came to determining age. Dr. Mark Lehner of the University of Chicago was quoted by the *New York Times* as saying that Professor Schoch was practicing pseudoscience. Dr. Zahi Hawass, Director of Antiquities of the Giza Plateau and Sakkara, dismissed Schoch's work as "American hallucinations."

Nobody wanted to know about a very early Sphinx.

10

IN 1994, French author Robert Bauval and his English collaborator Adrian Gilbert, published *The Orion Mystery.*[5] The book dealt with astronomical alignments found in the structures of the Giza plateau.

In the Great Pyramid, for example, there are four shafts, approximately eight inches square, two leading out of the King's Chamber, two out of the Queen's Chamber. The purpose of these shafts has puzzled Egyptologists for the better part of a century. They are sometimes referred to as ventilation ducts, although two of them did not reach the outer surface of the pyramid and could not have served this purpose.

In 1963, an American astronomer, Virginia Trimble, determined that the southern shaft in the King's Chamber was astronomically aligned on the constellation of Orion. The northern shaft of the King's Chamber had long been known to point toward the circumpolar stars while Bauval himself calculated that the southern shaft in the Queen's Chamber was aligned to the star Sirius.

These discoveries led Bauval to an examination not merely of the Great Pyramid, but of the entire three-pyramid group at Giza. He found the alignment and relative sizes of the three huge pyramids at Giza exactly matched the alignment and relative sizes of the three stars in Orion referred to as "Orion's Belt."

---

[5] Heinemann, London, 1994.

Furthermore, if the Milky Way was taken to represent the River Nile, then the angle of the pyramids in relation to the Nile exactly matched the angle of Orion's Belt in relation to the Milky Way. Bauval also discovered that two further pyramids at Abu Ruwash and Zawyat al Aryan also aligned precisely with the stars Saiph and Bellatrix in Orion.

These discoveries point to a considerable astronomical knowledge on the part of the Ancient Egyptians.

11

IN 1879, a native workman stumbled on an opening into the near-ruined Fifth Dynasty pyramid tomb of Unas, at Saqqara. Inside he found a series of hieroglyphic inscriptions. These Pyramid Texts, as the inscriptions became known, were subsequently described by R. O. Faulkner as "the oldest corpus of Egyptian religious funerary literature now extant."[6]

In 1952, Samuel B. Mercer, Professor of Semitic Languages and Egyptology at Toronto University, produced an English translation of the Texts that suggested they contained symbolic expression of actual astronomical observations.

The Pyramid Texts can be confidently dated to the Fifth Dynasty (since they were discovered in Fifth Dynasty tombs) but their content shows they relate to Fourth Dynasty times and possibly even earlier. This means that by c. 2613 BC at latest—the establishment of the Fourth Dynasty and the building of the first pyramids by the pharaoh Snefru—a sophisticated system of astronomy was in place in Ancient Egypt. A sophisti-

---

[6] In *The Ancient Egyptian Pyramid Texts,* Aris & Phillips, Warminster, 1993.

cated system of astronomy requires a long period of observation.

12

THE EGYPTIAN PRIESTHOOD expressed their astronomical records in mythic or religious terms. One myth Bauval and Gilbert examined for its astronomical content was the myth of the phoenix. They concluded that the phoenix, which was known in Egypt as the bennu bird, symbolized the recurring nature of time. Like a great many ancient peoples, the Egyptians believed in aeons, or cycles, of time that endlessly repeated throughout history. But this was not just a religious conviction: it was a belief based on astronomical observation.

A typical example of the way in which the Egyptians recorded their observations is found in the Egyptian *Book of the Dead*, a collection of funerary texts. This work specifically identifies the phoenix with the god Osiris. But Osiris was in turn identified with the constellation Orion. So by linking Osiris and the bennu bird the priest-astronomers were recording a cyclical aspect of this constellation. Modern astronomy tells us there really *is* a cyclical aspect of Orion.

13

PRECESSIONAL MOTION, also called the precession of the equinoxes, is the result of a wobble in the Earth's rotation. This causes our planet to describe a great slow circle over a prolonged period of years. Just as the Earth's daily rotation makes us see the sun rise and set (even though it does not actually move) so the precessional motion causes apparent changes in the position of the stars.

Although a full precession (which returns all constellations to their apparent starting points) takes 26,000 years, there is ample evidence the Ancient Egyptians were well aware of it. This does not mean they were watching the stars over that length of time, but it does make it likely that their observations spanned more than 2,000 years. They divided the zodiac into twelve parts and observed that it required 2,160 years for the precessional effect to complete itself in each part. Simple multiplication calculated the timing of a full circle as 25,920 years.

If the Egyptians' developed astronomy was in place by 2613 BC, and an aspect of it depended on 2,160 years of careful observation and record-keeping, then the very latest time they could begin the observation process was 4773 BC.

This was not a good time for astronomical observation. The Nabian Pluvial was in full swing. Egyptian skies were cloudy. The last time the Egyptians could study the stars as easily as they do today was prior to 12,000 BC.

∏ㄴ

    THE EGYPTIANS OBSERVED a cyclical motion of the constellations which they calculated as taking 25,920 years to complete. Since they associated the constellations with their gods, they decided that it took the gods 25,920 years to finish a full cycle of divine activity, before beginning their work anew at the point where they first started.

In conformity with the maxim "As above, so below" they concluded that the affairs of humanity must also follow a 25,920-year cycle, with less important subcycles of 2,160 and 72 years tending to bring less spectacular, but nonetheless important, recurrences.

According to Professor R. T. Rundle Clark, the phoenix was associated with two specific time periods—1,460 and 12,954 years. The first of these time periods relates to the star Sirius. The dawn rising of Sirius shifts by one day in every four years,[7] completing a full cycle in 1,460 years. The second is approximately half the precessional cycle of 25,920 years and as such marks the point of maximum apparent change in the position of a constellation.

Here we come to the crunch. The pyramid complex at Giza mirrors the constellation Orion in the night sky. Computer calculations show the alignments to be perfect at the time when the Great Pyramid was built, around 2450 BC. But the Pyramid Texts link the movements of Orion to a mythic Golden Age when Osiris and Isis were first sent to Earth to teach civilization to humanity. In other words, a specific position of Orion in the night sky marked the real beginnings of Egyptian civilization. Bauval and Gilbert concluded that the pyramid complex itself was designed, among other things, to record the date. Computer calculations show it could not have been later than 10,400 BC. If not then, it had to be 26,000 years earlier.

---

[7] For the same reason we add an extra day to February every Leap Year.

9 | WORSHIPING THE GODDESS

SINCE THE LATE nineteenth century archaeologists have unearthed more and more evidence that our prehistoric ancestors believed God was a woman. Such a belief seemed so bizarre that many of them had real difficulty interpreting the evidence of their own eyes. They began by inferring a "goddess cult" as if it were some localized aberration.

The viewpoint was supported by Scripture. The term "goddess" appears only five times in the Bible, with reference to just two incidents, one in the Old Testament, one in the New Testament.

The first of these (I Kings 11:5) describes how Solomon, despite his wisdom, "went after" Ashtoreth, the goddess of the Zidonians, thus doing evil in the sight of the Lord. The second tells how Demetrius, a silversmith, bemoaned the actions of the apostle Paul, who had been encouraging people not to buy temple statuary. The biblical account continues in Demetrius's words:

> So that not only this our craft is in danger to be set at nought; but also that the temple of the great goddess Diana should be despised, and her magnificence should be destroyed, whom all Asia and the world worshippeth.

And when they heard these sayings, they were full

of wrath, and cried out, saying, Great is Diana of the Ephesians.[1]

That phrase "whom all Asia and the world worshippeth" should have provided a clue, but didn't. Emphasis was placed on the cry "Great is Diana of the Ephesians" and the incident relegated to the level of a squabble among the citizens of Ephesus.

2

THE MIND-SET OF the early archaeologists extended into modern times. Even when examining Minoan Crete, where the evidence of a goddess culture is almost overwhelming, the rulers are invariably described as kings (although not a single representation of a king has yet been found). After more than fifty years of excavation on the island, archaeologist Nicolas Platon was forced to accept the participation of women in Minoan life, but decided this could only have happened "when their men folk were away at sea."

But as more evidence came to light, it became obvious that goddess worship was not a local cult, but a worldwide phenomenon. Still unable to imagine a culture so radically different to their own, archaeologists took to using terms such as "Earth Mother" and "fertility religion" that allowed them to view the goddess as only part of a broader religious picture. Even now, some textbooks refer to the predominant prehistoric religion in this way. Just how predominant is summed up by Riane Eisler:[2]

. . . the religion of the Great Goddess appears to have been the single most prominent and impor-

---

[1] Acts 19:27–28.
[2] Following quotes are taken from *The Chalice and the Blade*, Riane Eisler, HarperCollins, London, 1990.

tant feature of life. In the Anatolian site of Catal
Huyuk the worship of the Goddess appears to per-
meate all aspects of life. For example, out of 139
rooms excavated between 1961 and 1963, more
than 40 appear to have served as shrines.

This same pattern prevails in Neolithic and
Chalcolithic Europe. In addition to all the shrines
dedicated to various aspects of the Goddess, the
houses had sacred corners with ovens, altars
(benches) and offering places . . .

To say the people who worshipped the Goddess
were deeply religious would be to understate, and
largely miss, the point. For here there was no separation between the secular and the sacred. As religious historians point out, in prehistoric and, to a
large extent, well into historic times, religion was
life and life was religion.

In an analysis of Neolithic art, Eisler remarks:

Neolithic art reflects not so much an irrational as a
prerational world view. As contrasted to the more
empirical thinking so highly valued in our secular
age, it was the product of a mind characterized by a
fantasizing, intuitive, and mystical consciousness.

But "fantasizing, intuitive, and mystical" should not
be interpreted as "woolly." As Eisler points out, late
examples of goddess culture achievements, such as the
building of Avebury and Stonehenge, presuppose an advanced understanding of mathematics, astronomy, and
engineering.

The last island stronghold of goddess-oriented culture, Minoan Crete, had paved roads, indoor plumbing,
viaducts, architectural skills, navigational knowledge,
and a flourishing economy—material achievements

actually surpassing those of many developing cultures today. What really differed was emphasis. Says Eisler:

> . . . in these prehistoric . . . societies, technological advances were used primarily to make life more pleasurable rather than to dominate and destroy. This . . . points to the conclusion that, in this important respect, our earlier . . . societies were more evolved than the . . . societies of the present world, where millions of children are condemned to die of hunger each year while billions of dollars are poured into ever more sophisticated ways to kill . . . Increasingly, the work of modern ecologists indicates that this earlier quality of mind, in our time often associated with some types of Eastern spirituality, was far advanced beyond today's environmentally destructive ideology.

3

PLATO BELIEVED EGYPT—and indeed the city-state of Athens—came into being at a time when the religion of the Great Goddess was spreading (from heaven knows where) into the Mediterranean and North Africa. He quotes one of Solon's Egyptian priests as saying:

> I begrudge you not the story, Solon; nay, I will tell it both for your own sake and that of your city, and most of all for the sake of the Goddess who has adopted for her own both your land and this of ours and has nurtured and trained them . . .[3]

Eisler drew her detailed conclusions about a goddess culture from archaeological finds dating back, at

---

[3] Quoted from *Critias*, Plato.

their furthest reach, to about 7000 BC. But there is evidence that goddess worship was in place at an earlier period. A carved limestone statuette was discovered at Willendorf, Austria, in 1908. It was a four-inch-tall female figure, still showing traces of red pigment, with exaggerated breasts and hips. The heavy stress on female features have led experts to believe the statuette is a representation of the Great Goddess. The figure is dated to the Aurignacian period *c.* 30,000 BC, around the time when, according to the *Turin Papyrus*, the Horus-kings held sway in Ancient Egypt.

Since the discovery of the "Venus of Willendorf," as this little artwork came to be called, scores more goddess figurines have come to light. Their wide geographical spread is one indication of the extent of the goddess religion. One goddess figurine, discovered before the Willendorf Venus, is seldom mentioned in the standard texts of archaeology. It came from a well boring at Nampa, Idaho, in 1889. It was no more than an inch and a half long, a female figure that ". . . would do credit to the classic centers of art" according to G. F. Wright.[4] This figurine has been dated to the Plio-Pleistocene era, which makes it about 2 million years old. Not even the Ancient Egyptians believed their civilization reached back to that time. But it accords quite neatly with the idea that the earliest of our civilizations was a transplant from the planet Mars and raises a fascinating field of speculation.

To date, many of those tempted to discuss the sex of the face on Mars, have concluded it is male. The "platform" surrounding the face itself is often taken as a headdress, or even military helmet. The "diadem" which emerges on computer enhancement is seen as an indication that this is the portrait of a king.

---

[4] In his *Origin and Antiquity of Man*, Oberlin, 1912.

Yet such conclusions may be no more than the projection of a male-oriented culture. If the face is in fact female—and the "helmet" actually a styling of hair—then it becomes possible that Earth's ancient goddess religion literally came down from the heavens.

10 | ASTRONOMER PRIESTS

THE EVIDENCE OF Hapgood's maps points to the existence of a prehistoric civilization with a global reach. This civilization flourished in the Pleistocene, but we don't know how much earlier it was established. Plato suggests the prehistoric picture was not one of a single civilized state in an otherwise barbaric planet, but rather a number of civilized states at a more or less equal stage of development. These states included Egypt and Greece—or at least the ancient city-state of Athens.

The evidence of cave art shows there must also have been widespread hunter-gatherer communities during the Pleistocene, albeit with an unexpected amount of leisure, creative sophistication, and control over their environment. There was a unifying goddess-centered religion that seems to have extended across most cultural barriers, primitive and sophisticated.

Apart from the unifying religion, this picture of prehistoric culture is similar to the type of culture we have on Earth today. Although there are centers of advanced technical competence—up to and including space flight—in the West, the remainder of the world presents a spectrum of development that reaches all the way from Stone Age societies such as Botswana's Kung Bushmen and some Aboriginal tribes in Northern Australia to the electronic culture of industrialized Japan.

But so far, apart from a few questionable archaeological anomalies, there is no reason to suppose the peak of prehistoric civilization was anything as technically advanced as our own. On the evidence to date, it appears to have reached approximately the level of the classical civilizations familiar to every student of history.

2

THE SCOTTISH BARONET, Sir Charles Lyell, was one of the nineteenth century's most respected geologists. In *The Geological Evidence of the Antiquity of Man* he put the case against technically advanced prehistoric civilizations rather well. He wrote:

> If such civilizations existed, instead of the rudest pottery or flint tools . . . we should now be finding sculptured forms, surpassing in beauty the masterpieces of Phidias or Praxiteles; lines of buried railways or electric telegraphs, from which the best engineers of our day might gain invaluable hints; astronomical instruments and microscopes of more advanced construction than any known in Europe, and other indications of perfection in the arts and sciences.

Sir Charles was writing in 1863, thirteen years before the discovery of the wonderfully sophisticated cave art at Altamira, twenty-six years before the Nampa figurine that would have done credit to classical standards of art, and forty-five years before the delightful little Willendorf Venus turned up on the north bank of the Danube. He was also unaware of, or unimpressed by, those scraps of evidence such as metal nails and worked gold chains emerging from quarries and coal mines (see Chapter 4). But it would be boorish to deny his point.

If there really was a prehistoric culture established by an advanced spacefaring civilization, our archaeologists would be unearthing evidence of it in digs from here to Timbuktu. Unless something buried the evidence too deep for them to find.

3

AN OBVIOUS CANDIDATE would be the ending of the last Ice Age. According to the scientific consensus, the story of the Ice Age begins with the Pleistocene period, 2.5 million years ago. Ice sheets developed on highlands in North America and Europe then spread over the northern half of North America and a quarter of Eurasia. In short, ice came to dominate the Northern Hemisphere.

The wind intensified. Belts of westerlies were pushed toward the equator. Accelerated heat exchange produced more clouds and precipitation, both rain and snow. The Earth's surface became 1 to 2° C cooler. Glaciers spread over what is now the shallow sea floor of Hudson Bay and the Barents Sea. The older Antarctic and Greenland ice sheets grew larger. Mantles of ice developed in the group of mountain ranges stretching from southern Alaska to Colorado and California, in the European Alps, in the Ural and Caucasus mountains, and in the Himalayas.

Mountain glaciers in the Southern Hemisphere (in the South American Andes, the New Zealand Alps, and western Tasmania) extended down onto the plains.

Today, the Antarctic ice sheet is more than 8,000 feet thick. In central Greenland the ice reaches a thickness of 6,600 feet. The Pleistocene ice sheets were more than 10,000 feet thick in North America, and 8,200 feet thick in Europe.

As more and more of the planet's available water became locked in ice, sea levels fell. Ice Age seas were lower than today's by 330 to 460 feet, but with considerable fluctuations since the climate was far from static. During the last Ice Age, sea levels rose or fell more than 3 to 7 feet per century while ice crept over the land at

160 to 490 feet per year. When the Ice Age ended, sea
levels rose again.

L,

LOOK AT ANY global map that isolates
our major population centers. With only a few land-
locked exceptions, the great cities of the modern world
cling to the coastline. The list includes Adelaide, Aden,
Alexandria, Amsterdam, Athens, Bombay, Brisbane,
Cape Town, Casablanca, Dar es Salaam, Dublin, Havana,
Helsinki, Istanbul, Karachi, Kingston, Lima, London, Los
Angeles, Marseilles, Melbourne, Montevideo, New York,
Palermo, Perth, Port au Prince, Quebec, Rabat, Reykja-
vik, Rio de Janeiro, Shanghai, Stockholm, Sydney, Tel
Aviv, Tokyo, Vancouver, Wellington, and many, many
more.

There are clear-cut reasons for this. Ease of defense
and access to international shipping lanes encourages
the growth of coastal cities. If there really was an Ice
Age civilization as Charles Hapgood believed, it would
have been subject to the same strategic and commercial pressures. The maps suggest a maritime culture
and a maritime culture has its cities by the sea.

A rise in sea level following the retreat of the ice
would have devastated such a culture, inundating its
major cities and destroying age-old systems of trade
and commerce. This becomes particularly clear if you
examine a specific area. Although the *average* encroach-
ment of the sea at the ending of the Ice Age amounted
to less than 500 feet, there were areas where the inunda-
tion was considerably greater. At the height of the last
Ice Age, around 16,000 BC, for example, Greece had
coastal plains extending up to five miles. Yugoslavia
was connected to Italy while on the Aegean a plain
stretched westward from northern Anatolia to Thessaly.
Samothrace and Thasos were not the islands they are
today, but part of this sweeping landmass. There was a

further plain between Attica and Argolid, connections between Euboea and the mainland and even the Peloponnese and the mainland. All this land—and any settlements on it—was drowned by 7000 BC.

This is what's called a "best-case scenario." There have always been people who believed the destruction that followed the ending of the last Ice Age was far more extensive than the present scientific consensus allows.

5

PLATO'S ANCESTOR SOLON—the one the Egyptians told about Atlantis—was an Athenian statesman, known in Plato's day as one of the Seven Wise Men of Greece. At a time in the early sixth century BC, when Athens was on the edge of revolution, he introduced political reforms and a new Code of Laws he hoped would save the state. Nobody liked them. Solon became so unpopular—and so fed up trying to explain himself— that he left the country, undertaking to stay away for ten years to let things settle down. While he was on his travels, he made a point of visiting Egypt. Apart from politics, Solon's two great interests were poetry and history. It was this latter interest that drew him to Egypt. The North African civilization had a reputation for record-keeping that was unequaled in the ancient world. If you had an itch to find out about humanity's past, Egypt was the place to scratch it.

The keepers of the historical record were Egypt's priests. In the modern Western world, a priest is a cleric who has studied the scriptures of his religion and dedicated his life to its tenets. In the Orient, a priest may add the practice of spiritual disciplines like meditation or yoga. In Ancient Egypt, a priest was very different from either of these models.

One of the most immediate differences is that Egypt had an initiate priesthood. This means it functioned as a closed elite whose knowledge and practices were held secret to itself. In many ways, a member of the Egyptian priesthood was far closer to a modern scientist than a modern cleric. The priest was first and foremost an astronomer. It is now well established that he was a skilled mathematician[1] and had access to architectural and engineering techniques so advanced we might well envy them today. He was a healer with developed skills in medicine and possibly surgery. He was also an historian. His records were held in the temples.

6

THESE RECORDS INTERESTED Solon enormously but, ever the diplomat, he was reluctant to ask about them directly. Instead, he brought the conversation around to ancient history by relating Greek traditions on the subject. Among them was the legend of Deucalion and Pyrrha.

Deucalion was the king of Phthia in Thessaly, and Pyrrha's husband. When the god Zeus decided to destroy humanity by a flood, Deucalion built an ark in which he and Pyrrha survived the flood to land on Mount Parnassus. The similarities between this legend and the biblical story of Noah are obvious. Just as many Christians today accept that Noah's Ark was an historical reality, Solon believed the Deucalion legend referred, possibly poetically, to events that had actually occurred. He even tried to calculate their date. But a spokesman of the Egyptian priests interrupted him with the comment that the Greeks no longer had access to ancient tradition. According to this priest, humanity

---

[1] Despite the remarkable statement in one modern textbook that "The Egyptians were much less skilled in mathematics than were the Mesopotamians. Their arithmetic was limited to addition and subtraction, which also served them when they needed to multiply and divide. They could cope with only simple algebra . . ."

had been nearly wiped out not once, as in the story of Deucalion's flood, but many times. When this happened, detailed records of life before each disaster were lost and even memories soon faded. All that remained were distorted myths. The priest then specifically mentioned one of these myths, the story of Phaethon, a son of the sun god Helios.

When Phaethon was taunted about his illegitimacy, Helios promised him anything he wanted in order to prove his paternity. Phaethon asked to drive the sun chariot through the heavens for a single day. Helios permitted him to do so, but Phaethon could not control the vehicle, which came too near the Earth and began to scorch it. To prevent further damage, Zeus hurled a thunderbolt at Phaethon, who fell to Earth at the mouth of the Eridanus River. The Egyptian priest claimed, "That story as it is told has the fashion of a legend, but the truth of it lies in the occurrence of a shifting of the bodies in the heavens which move around the Earth and a destruction of the things on the Earth by fierce fire, which recurs at long intervals."[2]

In other words, it was a distorted account of an actual astronomical event that triggered mass destruction on our planet. Two-and-a-half thousand years later a Russian-born scholar, Immanuel Velikovsky, was trying to tell us much the same thing.

---

[2] In *Critias*, Plato.

11 | MOVING MOUNTAINS

DR. VELIKOVSKY HAD fearsome academic credentials. He studied in the universities of Moscow, Berlin, Vienna, and Edinburgh, and was for three years partnered with Albert Einstein in editing the *Scripta Universitatis atque Bibliothecae Hierosolymitarum* that laid down the foundation of the Hebrew University. He was awarded his M.D. in 1921 and practiced medicine in Palestine. During the 1930s, he studied psychology in Zürich and Vienna.

Velikovsky was attracted to the catastrophe model of human history that suggests change is not always gradual but is sometimes directed by massive natural disasters. Like the old priest of Sais, he thought distorted memories of such disasters were recorded in ancient myths. In 1950 he published his findings in a work called *Worlds in Collision*. He claimed the planet Venus had been ripped from the body of Jupiter in relatively recent times and careered in an erratic orbit around the solar system causing gravitational and magnetic havoc on Earth. The book, which was unusually readable for the work of an academic, became both a literary sensation and an international bestseller.

Although his theory led him to make certain predictions that were subsequently verified, critics questioned the plausibility of the celestial events described and the mechanisms he proposed to account for them. The consensus was that he had pushed his evidence over a cliff and his reputation lay shattered at the bottom.

The scientific community reacted as violently as Velikovsky's Venus. A threatened boycott of scientific textbooks produced by Macmillan, his original publisher, led to the transfer of rights to Doubleday after only two months of publication. The scientists claimed they disapproved of Velikovsky's methodology.

2

WHAT ARE NOW called glacial erratics were first noticed in the Jura Mountains in the form of immense granite boulders resting on the native limestone. During the eighteenth and nineteenth centuries, scientists began to argue about how they got there. At the time, the consensus position was typified by a professor of physics and philosophy at the Academy of Geneva, Horace Bénédict de Saussure, who concluded they had been swept to their present positions by torrents of water . . . the result of the Biblical Flood.

In 1837 another Swiss, the zoologist and paleontologist Louis Agassiz, put forward an alternative theory that the boulders had been carried not by water, but by ice. The idea was not well received but in 1840, Agassiz published his *Études sur les Glaciers (Studies of Glaciers)*, that showed Alpine glaciers had been far more extensive in the past. He went on to collect firm evidence of an Ice Age in Scotland, northern England, Ireland, and North America. Agassiz believed the onsets of his Ice Ages were both abrupt and catastrophic. In *Études* he wrote:

> The surface of Europe previously adorned with tropical vegetation and populated by herds of huge elephants, enormous hippopotami, and gigantic carnivora, was suddenly buried under a vast mantle of ice, covering plains, lakes, seas, and plateaux. Upon the life and movement of a vigorous creation fell the silence of death . . .

In an attempt to gain support for his ideas, Agassiz took the Dean of Westminster to Scotland. The Dean at the time was Dr. William Buckland, a pioneer geologist who had made one of the world's very first dinosaur finds. Buckland also believed in prehistoric catastrophes—notably the Biblical Flood—and was quickly convinced of Agassiz's theory by the evidence of Scottish glacial moraines.

Buckland, in turn, set out to convert Sir Charles Lyell, the same geologist who argued with such conviction against a prehistoric civilization. Lyell's reputation stood so high that his support virtually assured the acceptance of any theory.

Like Agassiz, Buckland decided on a field trip and showed Lyell a cluster of moraines less than two miles from his father's home. Lyell realized at once that the theory of an Ice Age solved a great many geological problems. In October 1840, Dr. Buckland was able to write to Agassiz that "Lyell has adopted your theory *in toto*!"

But Lyell hadn't. Even though he read a paper at the Geological Society of London on 5 November 1840 supporting Agassiz's hypothesis, he had one serious reservation. He didn't like the idea of catastrophes. Ten years previously, Lyell had begun to publish his three-volume *Principles of Geology* in which he argued that geologic change was the result of an accumulation of small, gradual factors. This principle, known as uniformitarianism, was first put forward by another Scot, James Hutton, in the late eighteenth century. Hutton's view was that geologic phenomena can all be explained by observable processes that have operated at much the same gentle level over immensely long periods of time.

In backing Agassiz's Ice Age theory, Lyell quietly threw out the catastrophic aspect. His immense prestige eventually established a scientific consensus on uniformitarianism in general and a gradual, noncatastrophic Ice Age in particular. That consensus has remained rock solid right up to the present day. The only problem is the vast amount of evidence against it.

3

THE HIMALAYAS COMPRISE the highest mountain range in the world, towering more than five miles at the peak of Mount Everest. When Western paleontologists first investigated the region (in the nineteenth century), they discovered to their astonishment that the topmost reaches of Himalayan strata—including Everest itself—contained the skeletal remains of marine life. The inference is inescapable. These great mountains were once under water. The Himalayas became the highest mountains on Earth only during the Pleistocene period that ended just 10,000 years ago. They did so due to "intense uplift" of crystalline rocks.

If you were to dig beneath the suburbs of Paris, you would find (like geologists before you) gypsum deposits containing the remains of more than 800 marine species. Continue digging and you will reach a layer of clay that houses reptile bones and freshwater shells. The area on which Paris now stands was once under the sea . . . and before then, dry land as it is today. Much of France is like that. The sedimentary layers excavated by geologists show a sequence of no less than six changes between sea and land. Excavations in other European countries reveal essentially the same pattern. Most of the continent was once under water. So were parts of North America. The skeletons of two whales were found in a bog in Michigan. Bones of another turned up a little north of Lake Ontario in Canada in an area that is now 440 feet above sea level. More whale bones were found at Vermont and in the Montreal-Quebec area, both at heights of around 500 feet above sea level. During the original colonization of the United States, whale bones were found in such numbers in the Alabama soil that farmers made fences out of them.

Those whales pose a problem to the scientific consensus on uniformitarianism.

L

SCHOOLCHILDREN LEARN there are five oceans on the surface of the globe. Most of us grow up believing they have some sort of geographical reality. They haven't. The dividing lines between one ocean and another are as arbitrary as the political boundaries of many African countries, or our habit of dividing North and South America into two continents despite the fact they are both part of the same landmass—or were until the Panama Canal was dug. There is, in fact, a single interconnected body of water stretching over some two-thirds of the globe, known to oceanographers as the World Ocean. It even includes a few of what were once called the Seven Seas.

Whales are oceangoing mammals found throughout the World Ocean. Sometimes they beach themselves, but when you discover the remains of a whale 500 feet *above* sea level, you have to ask yourself how it got there. There seem to be only three possibilities:

1. It was deposited on high ground by a tidal wave and subsequently died.
2. The ocean floor suddenly erupted upward (through, for example, volcanic action) carrying the whale with it and stranding the creature on newly created land.
3. The whale died peacefully, depositing its bones on the ocean bed which then elevated over millions of years to become dry land.

The uniformitarian consensus plumps for the last of these three options. But geologists also insist that the most recently formed areas of North America were above water at least 530 million years ago. That was more than 450 million years before the whales evolved.

5

WHALES AREN'T THE only problem. If anything, mammoths pose even greater difficulties. Mammoths are a type of elephant that flourished for more than a million years just about everywhere during the Pleistocene period, but became extinct with the ending of the Ice Age. In accordance with the doctrines of uniformitarianism, the extinction came about because the higher temperatures changed the habitat and these great creatures were unable to adapt.

What mitigates against this picture is that the higher temperatures changed the habitat *for the better*. We've already seen how the retreat of the glaciers led to increased rainfall and the spread of forest and grassland. All elephants are vegetarian and the mammoth was no different. On the face of it, the ending of the Ice Age should have encouraged its spread, not its extinction. Unless, of course, the Ice Age didn't end as gently as the uniformitarians believe.

6

THE TANANA VALLEY lies north of Mount McKinley in Alaska. There, as in other areas of Alaska, excavations several miles in length and up to 140 feet deep have revealed a morass of bones and timber that still ticks like a time bomb waiting to blow the uniformitarian consensus apart. The excavations were not made by geologists, but by a highly mechanized mining industry seeking to reach gold-bearing gravel beds below. Nonetheless, they are of enormous interest and importance to geologists. This permanently frozen layer of Alaskan soil contains the remains of millions upon millions of mammoth, mastodon, and super-bison, along with animals such as horses that are not extinct.

Mixed in with the frozen bones are millions of up-rooted and splintered trees. F. C. Hibben of the University of New Mexico is under no illusions about what happened:

> There is ample evidence that at least portions of this material were deposited under catastrophic conditions. Mammal remains are for the most part dismembered and disarticulated . . . twisted and torn trees are piled in splintered masses.[1]

The deaths of these animals have been dated to the end of the last Ice Age, approximately 10,000 years ago. This was no localized disaster. Similar deposits have been found on the lower reaches of the Yukon, on the Koyukuk and Kuskokwim rivers and along the Arctic coast. The Liakhov Islands in the Arctic Ocean seem to be composed entirely of mammoth bones held together by frozen sand. The New Siberian Islands, Stolbovoi Island and Belkov Island are jam-packed with mammoth and rhinoceros remains. Mammoth tusks have been dredged in huge quantities from the bottom of the Arctic Ocean. Since 1797 when the first such find was made, several mammoths have been discovered fully preserved in the Siberian ice.

There is very little about this picture that makes sense. The mammoths shouldn't have been living in the Arctic in the first place. An African elephant will consume 200 kilos of vegetation a day. The larger mammoth might be expected to eat even more. The vegetation to support them simply doesn't exist in the Arctic—at least not now. The vast amount of splintered timber mixed up with the bones suggests extensive for-

---

[1] Quoted from Hibben's paper *Evidence of Early Man in Alaska* in *American Antiquity*, Vol. 8, 1943.

estation. But our current picture of the Ice Age is one of glaciers that gradually extended from an already frozen north.

So if the North was frozen, several million mammoths, rhino and other animals, along with whole forests of trees must have been carried into the area from somewhere else. They must have been carried at the same time, all jumbled together, in a catastrophe that paralyzes the imagination. But this picture, which suggests some unbelievable tidal wave or planetary typhoon doesn't hack it either. Some of the preserved mammoths are uninjured and have undigested grasses in their stomachs. They were not carried by tidal waves or blown by typhoons. They were flash frozen where they stood.

7

SIBERIA IS TODAY the coldest place on Earth. It is not generally realized outside of scientific circles that it never had an Ice Age. Early explorers noted whole forests of petrified trees consisting of carbonized trunks. A glacier is essentially a river of ice. It would have razed them to the ground. There is no sign of a moving ice sheet in Siberian rock strata either. This is only one peculiarity of our northlands.

Fossil remains of magnolia and fig have been discovered in the north of Greenland. These plants require not only heat but light. Northern Greenland has a six-month Arctic night. There are coal seams in the Spitsbergen Archipelago. Coal is the result of geological pressures on ancient forests and other vegetation, turning them first into peat bogs, then into coal seams. In Spitsbergen, these ancient forests were growing only 8° 15′ from the North Pole. Tropical coral growths have been found in the chill polar seas around Canada, Greenland, and Alaska. There are signs of similar extreme climatic change elsewhere. Agassiz himself found ice scour in

Brazil. Argentina had its own Ice Age, as did British Guiana, India, Madagascar, and tropical Africa. The Indian and African ice sheets moved in the wrong direction. All the geological evidence is that they originated at the equator and moved north. In India the movement was not only north but uphill, into the lower reaches of the Himalayas. Since this is plainly impossible, the experts decided these signs related not to the last Ice Age, but to a much earlier one, millions of years ago in the Permian. But they don't explain why equatorial ice was less impossible then than later.

8

IN PARTS OF Britain, fossil flora indicates a temperate climate, but the bones of contemporary animals show an utterly inexplicable jumble of cold-weather and tropical species. Elephants, tigers, and hippopotami apparently rubbed shoulders with reindeer, elk, wolf, and bear. A similar mixture has been found in France and, to a more limited degree, Spain.

9

IN 1953, Professor Hapgood—the same Professor Hapgood who studied the maps of the ancient sea kings—put forward a comprehensive solution to this multitude of mysteries. He called it the theory of global crust displacement.

Then, as now, the scientific consensus supported meteorologist Alfred Wegener's concept of continental drift. Back in 1910, Wegener noticed how the outlines of various continents fitted together like an exploded jigsaw and decided they must once have formed a single supercontinent he called Pangaea. Although he couldn't quite figure out the driving force, he theorized that they got to their present positions by drifting slowly apart.

European geologists like the idea, and in England Arthur Holmes proposed that convection of the mantle—the part of the Earth's interior that lies underneath the crust—would provide the driving force for drift. Everybody liked that too.

Professor Hapgood accepted the reality of continental drift but put forward the idea that there were widely separated periods during which not just the continents, but the entire planetary crust moved . . . and moved significantly. These sudden shifts, that did not affect the axis or rotation of the planet, meant that previously temperate or even tropical regions could be carried into the Arctic or Antarctic circles, causing an abrupt plunge in temperatures and wiping out whole categories of warm-weather plants and animals. At the same time as temperate regions moved into the cold, frozen areas were shifted into the warm. As a direct result, vast quantities of ice quickly melted, causing a dramatic rise in sea levels throughout the globe.

Crustal displacement, in Hapgood's theory, was neither gradual nor smooth. It was accompanied by violent earthquakes and gigantic tidal waves, causing mass destruction and mass extinctions. The last period of crustal displacement, he suspected, marked the ending of the Ice Age.

Hapgood discussed his ideas with Albert Einstein, who loved them. He told Hapgood that gradualist notions common to geology were only a habit of mind and not necessarily justified by observable data. Einstein was so impressed he lent his name to the theory by contributing a foreword to Hapgood's book on the subject.[2]

Despite this endorsement, the theory was roundly ignored by the scientific community. Change was acceptable only so long as it was nice and gradual. All the

[2] *The Earth's Shifting Crust: A Key to Some Basic Problems of Earth Science*, Pantheon Books, New York, 1958.

same, the evidence that convinced Hapgood and Einstein is more than enough to suggest that if there was a technically advanced civilization on this planet much more than 11,000 years ago, most of its traces would have been obliterated by the massive changes as the Ice Age ended. But you'd imagine *some* hi-tech traces would remain.

12 | TEMPLES TO
THE STARS

THE ELDERLY PRIEST at Sais went to some pains to explain to Solon how it was that Egypt held records dating back to ancient times when other states did not. He maintained that there were two types of planetary disaster. One was caused by "fiery" astronomical phenomena such as meteor bombardment. The other came about through water, in the form of widespread flooding.

In times of fiery disaster from the skies, said the priest, "all they that dwell in the mountains and in high and dry places suffer destruction more than those who dwell near the sea." When, on the other hand, the disaster was caused by flooding, "all the herdsmen and shepherds which are in the mountains are saved, but those in the cities of your land are swept into the sea by the streams."

But Egypt, because of its peculiar geography, was well placed to survive either type of disaster. In fiery times, "the Nile, our Savior in other ways, saves us also at such times by rising high." When the great rains started, by contrast, "in our country neither then nor at any other time does the water pour down over our fields from above, on the contrary it all tends naturally to well up from below. Hence it is for these reasons that what is here preserved is reckoned to be the most ancient."

These ideas sound naive, but the fact remains that there is now hard evidence of a Pleistocene civilization such as the priests described and some support for their assertion that the Egyptian civilization dated to much earlier times than our present orthodox consensus allows. There is ample evidence of a developed science of astronomy in Ancient Egypt—so developed, in fact, that it would have required a lengthy period of conscientiously recorded observations to put it in place. Record-keeping requires writing, which must consequently have been in place in predynastic times.

Intensive archaeological work throughout the Nile Valley has produced no evidence of Egyptian civilization prior to about 3100 BC. This has led many Egyptologists to deny the possibility of a more ancient Egyptian culture and ignore the evidence that supports it. The real bugbear seems to be Lyell's tenacious doctrine of uniformitarianism, that only allows gradual change and a linear evolutionary progression from the simple to the complex, the primitive to the sophisticated. But if the ending of the last Ice Age precipitated a global disaster that caused the sudden downfall of any prehistoric culture, a wholly new picture can emerge. This is the picture of a proto-Egypt, on the Nile or elsewhere, as advanced as, or possibly even more advanced than, the Egypt of classical times.

Such a civilization would have been all but destroyed at the ending of the Ice Age, but as the old priest suggested, specific geographical conditions might have allowed a concentration of survivors in the Nile Valley, preserving some skills and certain ancient records. After a period of barbarism, the descendants of these survivors would finally have *reestablished* their civilization, drawing on the preserved continuity of their records, around 3100 BC.

The experience of Europe in the Middle Ages shows how easily a culture can fall into long periods of decline even without a global disaster to contend with. But so long as some of the old records are preserved, the possibility of a renaissance is always there. Such a renaissance produces a culture radically different to that which immediately preceded it but with telltale signs of influence from a more distant and more advanced age. Such telltale signs are present in the historical civilization of Ancient Egypt.

2

A HISTORY OF weaponry in the *Grolier Electronic Encyclopedia* records that

> . . . the Assyrians (2000–612 BC) . . . used bows and arrows, swords, maces (spiked clubs), battle-axes, spears, shields, and scale armor. The Assyrians also conducted masterful sieges and excelled in the art of fortification. Another culture, the Chaldeans, used cavalry by about 1000 BC.

The Greeks, Romans, Chinese, Goths, and Vikings all played their part in the development of major instruments of destruction. The Egyptians do not even rate a passing mention.

But if retarded in weaponry, the Egyptians were advanced in other areas to an almost unimaginable degree. In every case, the implication is that they drew their inspiration from a tradition far older than the orthodox establishment of their dynastic state.

3

WHEN PROFESSOR LIVIO Catullo Stecchini was still a student, he came across something extremely disturbing.

> I was gradually forced to accept the fact that scholars of ancient history do not read numbers, neither in ancient texts nor in research papers. I noticed a number of times when I submitted a paper for judgment by a specialist of a particular area that he

would quickly turn a page if he saw numbers on it. In many different guises I was told that "numbers do not constitute evidence in ancient studies."[1]

The attitude had practical implications. When Stecchini submitted his thesis on "The Origin of Money in Greece" it was accepted as containing much of value, but he was strongly advised that before publishing it he should "cut down on all those numbers."

Despite his irritating insistence on examining the numbers, Stecchini eventually managed to obtain his doctorate in ancient history at Harvard. He received it for a thesis on ancient measures. Since then he has applied much of his skill in numbers to investigating the level of mathematical, geographical, geometrical, and geodetic[2] knowledge in Ancient Egypt. In each case he found it to have been astonishingly advanced.

Stecchini made a study of the same hieroglyphic texts as other Egyptian scholars, but took care not to skip the numbers. The approach paid dividends. It showed, for example, that as long ago as the unification of their country—and quite possibly much earlier—the Egyptians knew the length of the circumference of the Earth.[3] They could measure latitude and longitude to an accuracy of a few hundred feet. They knew the length of their country to the nearest cubit. They were aware of every important geographical coordinate in their land from the Mediterranean to the equator.

---

[1] Quoted from *Notes on the Relation of Ancient Measures to the Great Pyramid* published as an Appendix to *Secrets of the Great Pyramid* by Peter Tompkins, Allen Lane, London, 1973.
[2] This unusual term refers to the placement of markers related to geographical and sometimes even terrestrial absolutes.
[3] With the implication that they knew it was a sphere—a fact which did not dawn on Europeans until the fifteenth century.

Texts published by the German Egyptologist Ludwig Borchardt give the length of Egypt from the First Cataract of the Nile to Behdet on the Mediterranean as 106 *atur*. An atur is 15,000 royal cubits, which translated into modern measure gives a distance of 831,240 meters. From this, it is possible to calculate the figure the Egyptians placed on a degree of latitude—110,832 meters. Modern science believes the actual figure to be 110,800 meters, a minute difference of only 0.032 of a meter. Calculations of the average degree of latitude between the equator and the pole resulted in a figure of 111,136.7 meters. Today's estimate is 111,134.1 meters.

According to Stecchini, a prime meridian was established by Egyptian geographers exactly dividing the country in two longitudinally. In order to simplify geography, cities and temples were deliberately sited at distances expressed in round figures, or at worst very simple fractions, from this prime meridian or a calculated Tropic of Cancer. The predynastic capital, Behdet, was actually built on the prime meridian, as was the new capital of Memphis.[4] The heretical pharaoh, Akhenaten, returned to the oldest of measures and established *his* new capital exactly halfway between Syene on the Tropic and Behdet. Boundary stones were set to an accuracy of one in 10,000.

Stone markers, known as *omphaloses*, were placed at specific geodetic centers, marked with meridians and parallels and showing the distance to other *omphaloses*. As in Egyptian astronomy, geography and geodesy were inextricably associated with worship of the gods. The *omphalos* of Thebes was placed in the temple of Amon, at the precise spot where meridian and parallel crossed.

So advanced were the geographers of Egypt that their country actually became the geodetic center of

---

[4] The geodetic point which determined the siting of Memphis was called Sokar, after the god of orientation.

the ancient world. Capitals of many countries were sited with reference to the Egyptian meridian—including the ancient Chinese capital of An-Yang. Delphi in Greece, the Moslem Mecca, and the original religious center of Judaism at Mount Gerizim, all owe their location to the original work of the Egyptians.

The system, allied to a stylized geography so ingeniously simple that it could be remembered without the need of maps, meant the citizens of Egypt could travel their country without the likelihood of getting lost. Religious sites became accessible to all and trade flourished. But there is one other important implication of Stecchini's discoveries. Egypt, as far back as predynastic times, was built in accordance with this great geodetic system—which must mean the system itself was fully worked out at a *prior* time. What we have here is not a country that grew in the organic fashion of later European states, with cities established by reason of natural resource, defense, or trade. It was a country that was *preplanned*. Its planners must have learned their skills from an earlier era.

L

IF THE ASTRONOMICAL and geographic knowledge of the Ancient Egyptians was impressive, their architectural and engineering skills were positively awesome.

When Sir Norman Lockyer, the British astronomer and Egyptologist, first saw the temple of Amon-Ra at Karnak he was moved to describe it as "beyond all question the most majestic ruin in the world." Generations of tourists would share his sentiment. The site features avenues of ram-headed sphinxes, towering pillars, and immense colossi. Columns in the great halls soar to a height of twenty meters and are more than three meters in diameter. Papyrus texts indicate that in its heyday, it employed 2,100 people responsible for 65 villages, 83 ships, 403 gardens, 20,000 square meters of cultivated land, and 500,000 head of livestock. This sort of scale was not unusual.

Cleopatra's Needle, in reality a Heliopolis obelisk dating to the reign of Thutmose III, now towers above London's Thames Embankment to a height of some 21 meters. An obelisk ordered by Queen Hatshepsut around 1500 BC was 30 meters in height. The Colossus of Memnon near Thebes, actually two enormous statues in the image of Amenhotep III, was so large it was revered through the ancient world. The funerary temple of Hatsheput in the Theban necropolis literally integrates outcrops of the surrounding mountain.

In October 1850, the great Egyptologist Auguste Mariette discovered a sphinx half buried in the sand at Saqqara. It proved to be one of a number lining a lost avenue that led to the Memphis Serapeum recorded centuries before by Strabo. This underground labyrinth, that contained the mummified bodies of Apis bulls, was among the most spectacular discoveries of archaeology. One subsequent visitor remarked:

> It is impossible to imagine the impression created by this vast underground passageway . . . Leading off the gallery are lateral chambers housing the immense sarcophagi of the Apis bulls . . . whichever way you turn, the effect is truly magical.[5]

The sarcophagi were three meters high, two meters wide, and four meters long, each one carved out of a single block of granite with its surface polished mirror smooth. Jean François Champollion, the French scholar who became the first to decipher hieroglyphic script in 1822, went on record with the comment that "no other people, whether in antiquity or nowadays, ever con-

---

[5] Quoted by Jean Vercoutter in *The Search for Ancient Egypt*, Thames & Hudson, London, 1992.

ceived the art of architecture on such a gigantic scale."
Quite how gigantic was highlighted by a sequence of
events that began in 1956, the year the Egyptian government decided to construct a new dam at Aswan.

5

ALTHOUGH BELIEVED NECESSARY for the
country's agricultural prosperity, the plan to build the
second Aswan Dam was seen as a cultural disaster. The
site included some of the most spectacular monuments
of ancient times.

Urged on by a UNESCO appeal launched in 1960, an
outraged world community funded a rescue project. In
the eight years remaining before the building of the
dam, forty archaeological expeditions descended on the
area and more than twenty monuments were saved, including the rock-hewn temples of Abu Simbel.

These temples were built on the orders of Rameses II
in 1260 BC. The smaller of the two, designed as a sanctuary of the goddess Hathor, commemorated the pharaoh's wife Nefertari, and was adorned with several
statues that were each some 10 meters high, or roughly
the height of a modern three-story building.

But this was a doll's house by comparison with what
is now referred to as the Great Temple. Four colossal
statues of Rameses, measuring about 20 meters high,
were hewn from solid rock to provide its facade. Their
heads alone were more than four meters broad. The
ears were so large a man could actually sit inside them.
Gigantic hands, measuring 2.64 meters, rest on massive
knees. Each eye is 0.84 of a meter in size, each nose 0.98
of a meter long. The temple's inner chambers and chap-
els extended back more than 60 meters into the heart of
the mountainside.

The scheme designed to save these two great temples involved literally cutting them to pieces, transport-
ing them to higher ground, and reassembling them on a

site safe from the waters of the dam. Teams of workmen sawed the monuments into 1,047 blocks, each weighing somewhere between 20 and 30 tons. A further 7,700 blocks of similar weight were required to move their immediate surrounds.

While these figures indicate the scale of the temples—which are by no means the largest structures in Egypt—they give no hint of the sophistication that went into their construction. First, they were ornately decorated and painted, with bas reliefs showing the life of the people and the military successes of the pharaoh. Lifesize statues of the queen and her children were cut near the colossi and inside the building. But most impressive of all was the orientation of the Great Temple.

6

THE ANCIENT ARCHITECTS and priest-astronomers designed the structure in such a way that twice a year, in February and October, the rays of the rising sun would travel through a colonnaded hall to penetrate an inner sanctum that was lightless the rest of the year. There they would illuminate statues of Amun, Ra-Harakti, and Rameses himself, while leaving in darkness a fourth statue depicting Ptah, Lord of the Underworld. This subtlety of alignment was not unusual.

Sir Norman Lockyer, who was so impressed by the Temple of Amon-Ra, discovered that its axis was accurately oriented to the summer solstice. It was just one of many such finds. Along the length of the Nile, Lockyer came upon temple after temple with solar (and even stellar) alignments. The longer the axis of a given temple, the narrower the beam of sunlight would be. The idea, Lockyer decided, was to measure the exact moment of a solstice. Egypt's architects and engineers had, in the words of Lockyer, created at Karnak and elsewhere "a scientific instrument of very high precision, as by it the length of the year could be determined with the greatest possible accuracy."

When a temple has a solar alignment, it will function with only slight loss of accuracy for up to 6,000 years. Stellar alignments are far less permanent. The precession of the equinoxes will cause a stellar temple to cease useful function in two or three centuries. But this presented few problems to the ancient engineers. They simply realigned the axis or rebuilt the temple. The temple at Luxor has no less than four well-defined alignment changes. Lockyer's measurements showed several Karnak temples had been changed to match the precessional changes in their aligned stars. So widespread was the practice that most pharaonic and all Ptolemaic temples were reconstructed at one time or another.

Lockyer found temples oriented toward Ursa Major, Capella, Antares, Phact, and Alpha Centauri, as well as alignments to Orion and Sirius. Work on two Ptolemaic temples convinced Lockyer they had been rebuilt, probably more than once, over a time period that certainly went back as far as 700 BC and quite possibly reached into the Fourth Dynasty of the Old Kingdom.

On the basis of astronomical data, Lockyer revised the dates of the Fourth Dynasty to 3733 BC, 600 years earlier than the orthodox estimate of the beginnings of the Egyptian state. Both temples were dedicated to goddesses—Isis and Hathor. Unencumbered by the orthodoxy that dated Egyptian civilization to 3100 BC, he decided the Isis temple had been oriented to Dubhe in 4000 BC and Gamma Draconis 1,000 years earlier. He believed the ancient architects had created temples that aligned toward Canopus prior to 6400 BC. He considered there was ample evidence of astronomical knowledge and engineering ability in Egypt well into predynastic times, but dropped an academic bombshell with the opinion that "the Great Pyramids were built by a new invading race." This race, he said, clearly brought with them an *advance* in astronomical thought.

13 | THE PYRAMID MYSTERY

WHATEVER HEIGHTS WERE reached in the construction of the ancient temples, even these were surpassed by the extraordinary feats of engineering that went into the Egyptian pyramids.

To most people, the pyramids of Egypt mean the three huge structures on the Giza plateau close to modern Cairo. But there are traces of at least 100 pyramids in Egypt, some 80 of them still visible, although many are in ruins. Most date from the Old Kingdom (c. 2686–2181 BC) and are located within a 100-kilometer strip of the Nile's west bank, between Hawara and Abu Ruwaysh.

The oldest known pyramid is the Step Pyramid of King Zoser at Saqqara, estimated to have been built c. 2650 BC. The plans were drawn up by Imhotep, an architect of such exalted reputation that he was considered a god by the Egyptians and a myth by many Egyptologists. His statue, in black dorite, shows a slim, almost frail little man with a disproportionately large head and sensitive features.

Zoser's pyramid has a large *mastaba*[1] as its nucleus and consists of six terraces of diminishing sizes, one built upon the other. It was surrounded by an elaborate complex of buildings, now partially restored. The next phase of development was the 93-meter-high pyramid at

---

[1] The name given to rectangular superstructures, common in the Old Kingdom, used for tombs. The word is Arabic and means "bench."

Maydum, built at the order of Snefru, founder of the Fourth Dynasty around 2613 BC. It seems to have been designed as a step pyramid, but later the steps were covered with a smooth stone facing to produce sloping sides. An interesting pyramid at Dashur was also built by Snefru. Halfway between its base and apex its inclination was changed, so that it is bent in appearance. The largest pyramids, built during the Fourth Dynasty, are found at Giza. The pyramid of Khufu (Cheops), believed to have been built about 2500 BC, is the largest of all.

A characteristic feature of most classical Egyptian pyramids is a temple complex, comprising a lower or valley temple at a short distance from the pyramid connected by a causeway to a second temple next to the pyramid. At Giza the temples have disappeared, with the exception of a well-preserved granite valley temple of Khafre (Chephren).

The last major pyramid of the Old Kingdom is that of Pepi II of the Sixth Dynasty (c. 2345–2181 BC). Almost no further pyramids were built until the Eleventh Dynasty pharaoh Mentuhotep II came to power in 2060 BC. During the Eleventh and Twelfth Dynasties until 1786 BC, pyramids continued to be built at Dashur and al-Faiyum, but later the custom died out completely. One of the most interesting things about Egyptian pyramids is that the more recent examples are the most poorly built.

2

SOME EXPERTS HAVE argued for a steady improvement in building techniques from the time of King Zoser onward, but when sophistication peaked with the Giza complex, it was downhill all the way. Even the Fifth Dynasty pyramids (in which the pyramid texts were found) built less than a century later are now little

better than heaps of rubble, while their earlier counterparts still stand as wonders of the world.

It is difficult to understand why such a dramatic degeneration occurred in so short a time, but there is one
possibility. In Ancient Egypt, scientific knowledge,
which was not differentiated from religious knowledge,
and its attendant technology was the exclusive preroga-
tive of an elite, initiate priesthood. All the evidence
points to the fact that a portion of this knowledge (perhaps even a major portion) was not the result of observation and experiment, but was inherited from an
earlier culture.

Inherited knowledge has certain drawbacks. One is
that it is not always understood by those who inherit it.
Another is that the body of accumulated knowledge
eventually exceeds the investigative abilities of the
small initiate group. What this comes down to is that if a
majority of initiates are interested in, say, astronomy,
then astronomy will tend to be the branch of ancient
wisdom that is actively used and expanded. But the
concentration on astronomy means that correspond-
ingly less time is devoted to other disciplines.

3

SOMETHING SIMILAR OCCURS in our own
time. There are fashions in science as clear-cut as fashions in clothes. Fashionable projects attract most fund-
ing, with the result that breakthroughs are far more
likely to occur in these fields than in others. In initiate
science, where both information flow and the number of
scientists were far more restricted, the imbalance must
have been greatly exaggerated.

Against this background you might imagine a static
period in architecture and engineering that took a great
leap forward in the early years of the Old Kingdom because of the emergence of a small body of initiates with
architectural/engineering interest. It is even possible, as

the Egyptian texts themselves suggest, that the leap was occasioned by a single initiate of genius, Imhotep, who had the specialist wisdom necessary to understand advanced techniques handed down from the lost prehistoric civilization. His experience of the Zoser pyramid would have enabled him to test and modify his understanding.

If orthodox dating is correct, he could not have lived long enough to become personally involved in the building of the Giza pyramids. But it's possible, as tradition claims, that they were built to his plans. Since even orthodox dating allows no more than 150 years between the building of Zoser's pyramid and the Great Pyramid of Khufu, it requires a relatively small margin of error to allow the possibility that Imhotep may have been contemporary with them both.

In this context it is interesting to find that Sir Flinders Petrie, the doyen of early British Egyptologists, noted a puzzling mixture of accuracy and clumsiness in the construction of the antechamber of the King's Chamber in the Great Pyramid. A number of granite blocks appeared unfinished and some were positively defective. Petrie expressed the opinion that the original architect of the structure had stopped supervising his work.

L

THE PYRAMIDS OF Egypt represent a feat of engineering that is almost mind-numbing. Thirty million tons of material went into their construction, three-quarters of it concentrated into the brief historical time span of the Fourth Dynasty. The step pyramid of Zoser used 850,000 tons. The two pyramids built under the orders of Pharaoh Snefru at Dashur had a combined weight of 9 million tons.

But monstrous though such figures are, they shrink to insignificance when compared with the statistics of the Great Pyramid, known at the time of its building as the Horizon of Khufu. The base of this incredible construction covers 13 acres of bedrock. Around 2.5 million limestone and granite blocks went into its construction, each weighing between 2 and 70 tons. It rises more than 201 tiers to the height of a modern 40-story building. In its original form, the exterior was covered by 15-ton slabs of polished limestone (which, unlike marble, does not discolor with age) giving a total mass of 6.3 million tons. To put a figure like this into some sort of context, there is more stone in this one pyramid than in all the cathedrals and churches built in England over the past 2,000 years. Napoleon once calculated that by tearing down the pyramid he would have enough raw material to erect a wall three meters high and one meter thick around the whole of France.

But it is not only by reason of its size that the Great Pyramid is impressive. The bedrock platform on which it was erected was first artificially leveled to a tolerance of a fraction of an inch. The base, that has a perimeter of close to a kilometer, is square to an accuracy of 0.08 percent. The sides are aligned to the cardinal points to a tolerance of 0.06 percent. Casing stones, many tons in weight, have been set down so finely that a knife blade will not fit between them. There are two main chambers within the structure. In the uppermost of these, the so-called King's Chamber, the edges of granite blocks have been cut with optical precision. A skim of mortar has been so evenly applied that there is no deviation from 1/50 of an inch over a surface area of 35 square feet.

5

ARCHAEOLOGISTS SAY NEITHER the wheel nor the pulley existed in Ancient Egypt. There were no domesticated horses either. The pyramids were built by sweating human muscle which quarried blocks and dragged them, sometimes over long distances, using rollers, then lifted them by means of ramps.

The modern master builder Peter Hodges applied experience gained in the Royal Engineers during World War II and decided the ramp theory was ridiculous. Part of the problem was the sheer volume of material in the sort of ramps that would be needed. To give a realistic gradient of 1 in 10, the ramp required for Khufu's pyramid would have stretched beyond the Giza plateau into the surrounding foothills. It would have had a volume of 8 million cubic meters—far larger than the pyramid itself. Even a steeper—hence less practical—ramp of 1 in 7 gradient would have a volume of more than 5.2 million cubic meters.

Where did all this material go to when the building was finished? Certainly not into the nearby stone quarry, still visible today, which it would have filled completely. If you spread it about the site to a depth of ten meters, it would cover 140 acres. At a lesser depth, say the height of a man, it would cover 700 acres. There is no sign of this volume of material anywhere near Giza. The rubble discovered by archaeologists is consistent only with the natural wastage you would expect when dressing stone.

A second problem is the question of block flow. Using a single ramp—or anything up to four ramps for that matter—the massive stone blocks of the pyramid would have to arrive at the working plane at the rate of two a minute, without fail, for twenty years. There were other problems associated with ramps in Hodges' view, but the figures he calculated in relation to ramp volume and block flow were enough to put paid to the consensus theory.

6

FOR HODGES the mystery of pyramid building has already been solved by the Greek historian Herodotus who wrote quoting Egyptian sources:

> The method employed was to build it in steps, or as some call them, tiers or terraces. When the base was complete, the blocks for the first tier above it were lifted from ground level by contrivances made of short timbers; on this tier there was another, which raised the blocks a stage higher, then yet another which raised them higher still. Each tier or story had its set of levers, or it may be that they used the same one, which, being easy to carry, they shifted up from stage to stage as soon as its load was dropped into place. Both methods are mentioned, so I give them both here. The finishing off of the pyramid was begun at the top and continued downward, ending with the lowest parts nearest the ground.[2]

This description was available to generations of Egyptologists who, lacking experience in building, dismissed it to a man. To the master builder Hodges, it gave a precise and reasonable explanation of what must have happened. Says Hodges:[3]

> The true nature of the problem does not seem to have been properly understood . . . A stone is so dense that not enough men can get a purchase under it to effect a direct vertical lift . . . The use of a

---

[2] *The Histories*, Herodotus, trans. Aubrey de Selincourt, Penguin Books, London, 1974.
[3] In *How the Pyramids Were Built*, Element Books, Shaftesbury, 1989.

cradle with carrying handles can be discounted even for the average core stones . . . because these would have needed teams of over 70 men . . .

There are two distinct methods of raising any load; from above by hoisting or from below by lifting. This distinction is important because the Egyptians of the Fourth Dynasty, having no wheels, pulleys or cranes, instinctively tackled their heavy loads by lifting them upward from beneath . . .

While archaeologists think in terms of lifting huge stones hundreds of feet, Hodges points out that before this could be done, the real problem was lifting them through the first few inches. Finding out how this was done enables you to understand the remainder of the process. For Hodges, there was no question but that levers were used:

The Ancient Egyptians seem not to have had ratchets, but they could easily have inserted packing under the stone as the lever handles touched the ground, thus securing the maximum gain in lift before the levers were removed.

The use of manpower is by no means always inferior to mechanical power when heavy loads are to be moved. Experienced men working together as a team have a flexibility in the control of their power and an instant response to the needs of the moment.

Teams of men could quickly raise the stones from step to step up the pyramid. Timber packing would be inserted after each "jack" by boys working on the step below. The stones for the core weighed about two and a half tons and the teams would soon have brought their work to a fine rhythm,

raising a stone halfway up a pyramid in the space of
a day.[4]

Hodges was so convinced that the Egyptians had
"evolved a sophisticated control over the use of levers"
that he decided to put his theory to the test. It worked.

Using levers, it needed just two men to lift a two and
a half ton mass. Hodges calculated that four men, each
with a lever, would take only about ten pushes to raise
a standard block up one step of the pyramid. Heavier
stones would have required more levers and more
pushes, but could have been moved in exactly the same
way.

The Ancient Egyptians placed the great stones with
optical precision in this way. Their techniques, using
little more than muscle and ingenuity, were more accurate, more efficient, and vastly more economical than
anything today's machine-based building industry
could manage.

To judge from the structures at Cydonia, the ancient
Martians had developed skills in monumental engineering. Such skills would have been vested in the colonial
civilization they established on Earth in deep prehistory. It may be that the Egyptians inherited their techniques. If so, they were not the only ones.

---

[4] *Ibid.*

14 | THE PORT IN THE SKY

WHEN HERNAN CORTES and Francisco Pizarro first encountered the astounding cities of the Aztec and Inca civilizations, it must have seemed they had stumbled on lost Atlantis. But both Aztecs and Incas were relative newcomers to Central and South America.

According to their own legends, the Aztecs originated from a place called Aztlan. While the exact location of Aztlan has never been established, the Aztecs themselves placed it somewhere in north or northwest Mexico. At the time, they were a small, nomadic tribe, living on the border of civilized Mesoamerica. In the 1100s AD they began a 100-year period of wandering before settling in the central Mexican valley. Regional wars finally drove them to a small island in Lake Texcoco where, about 1345, they founded the town of Tenochtitlan. (The site is now occupied by Mexico City.) A second group of Aztecs settled on the nearby island of Tlatelolco, thirteen years later. Both sites began as small collections of reed huts but later developed into cities. They eventually combined to create a vast metropolis.

At the time they established Tenochtitlan, the Aztecs were ruled by Azcapotzalco, the greatest of the city-states in the valley. But in 1428 they defeated Azcapotzalco and established themselves as the dominant power in the region. By 1519—the year the Spaniards arrived—the combined Tenochtitlan-Tlatelolco city had a population of more than 150,000. It was laid out on a grid plan and covered more than 12 sq kilometers (4.6 sq miles).

At the center of Tenochtitlan was a large walled precinct containing the main temples, schools, and priests' quarters, a court for their ritual ballgame, a wooden rack holding the skulls of sacrificial victims, and many commemorative sculptures. Just outside the precinct walls were the royal palaces. A 16-kilometer (10-mile) dike sealed off part of the lake and controlled flooding, so that Tenochtitlan stood on an island in an artificial lagoon. Causeways linked the island to the lake shore, and canals reached to all parts of the city.

2

THE ORIGINS OF the Incas are far more obscure. The Spanish invaders heard and recorded an official Inca history, but were in no position to separate historical events from myth. Scholars now believe the Inca empire started out as a small kingdom during the fourteenth century AD. A powerful state, centered near what is now Ayacucho in Peru, had apparently controlled the area several centuries earlier, but by the tenth century smaller feuding kingdoms dominated the scene.

Historians think the Inca comprised one of these small kingdoms and gradually assumed supremacy over their neighbors. Manco Capac was the legendary founder of the royal dynasty that ultimately ruled the Inca empire. Tradition has it that he originally came from south of Cuzco and eventually established there the settlement that was to become the imperial capital. Legend says he was turned to stone, and preserved as one of the Inca's most revered religious objects.

The Incas, who were established at Cuzco after about 1250, began more extensive conquests in the early fifteenth century. They conquered the Chimu in the 1460s and their northward expansion was still in progress when the Spanish arrived. At that time, the Inca empire extended along the spine of the Andes from the River Maule in south-central Chile to the northern border of present-day Ecuador. By elaborate terracing and irrigation, the Inca cultivated the mountainside and erected amazing mountain citadels.

But if Incas and Aztecs were relatively recent arrivals, their roots ran deep.

Ǝ

THE SCIENTIFIC CONSENSUS accepts that humans first came to the Americas from Asia when a land bridge existed between Siberia and Alaska. Accepted archaeological findings indicate human habitation as far back as 30,000 years. Controversial finds point to a far longer period.

Plants were cultivated in Mesoamerica at least as early as 7000 BC, although foraging and hunting were still the most important sources of food. Traces of temporary camps left by small hunter-gatherer bands high in the mountains northwest of Guatemala City are the only firm indications of human occupation anywhere in the area before the third millennium BC. Inhabitants were producing finely woven cotton textiles by about 2500 BC. These inhabitants were the Maya, an Indian people who once occupied a solid block of territory extending through Mexico, Guatemala, Belize (the former British Honduras), Honduras, and El Salvador, including the lowlands of the Yucatan peninsula and the volcanic highland region to the south.

Ꮮ

THE FIRST HARD evidence of human activity in the lowlands comes from Cuello in northern Belize. A village of permanent timber frame thatched dwellings was evidently established there by 2500 BC and by 1500–900 BC an agricultural economy was fully developed. Cuello is the earliest known settled community anywhere in the Maya world, and the pottery manufactured there is the earliest found in Mesoamerica. Cuello's economy was mixed: hunting and plant collecting were still important, but farming made a major contribution to the diet. Comparable farming villages were established throughout the Maya world by about 1000 BC. Trade increasingly forged links among various Maya regions. Against this background there arose the first real civilization of the region—the Olmec culture of the southern Veracruz gulf coast. Its importance lies in the fact that many later Mesoamerican civilizations trace their ancestry to it.

5

WHAT IS NOW called Mayan culture was, in essence, Olmec. By 1200 BC, Olmec civilization was fully developed at San Lorenzo, but about 900 BC there was a shift in power to La Venta. Both cities were impressive. Massive engineering projects included clay building platforms, stone pavements, and sophisticated drainage systems.

Typical works of Olmec art were colossal basalt sculptures of human heads and portable jade carvings. Both were enormously difficult to produce. Huge numbers of people had to be organized to locate the rare types of stone needed, then to transport it to their capitals, and finally to spend the thousands of hours needed to shape and finish the work. Neither jade nor basalt was available where the Olmec centers were built. The former was carried from the state of Guerrero, far to the northwest and from Guatemala and Costa Rica, far to the southeast. Basalt blocks, each weighing several tons, came from the Tuxtla volcanic range, located far north of the Olmec sites. They were transported partially by rafts but were also dragged many miles over land. The hard, dense stone was painstakingly carved by skilled sculptors into colossal naturalistic portrait heads each weighing some twenty-four tons or into monumental, powerfully muscular seated figures. The facial characteristics of these heads are Negroid, as if the Olmec knew about African peoples.

6

THERE ARE FURTHER hints of links with Africa—and specifically with Ancient Egypt. Almost all power in Egypt was gathered in the hands of the initiate priesthood who determined the structure of the great ceremonial centers. In Central America, every impressive Mayan site was a ceremonial center.

The Olmec appeared as abruptly in Central America as Egyptian civilization did in the Nile valley. What is usually put forward as their starting point—1200 BC—actually represents a culture as fully formed and advanced as that of the pharaohs. The Olmec were responsible for great intellectual achievements, including a system of writing and a precise calendar based on a high level of mathematics. So were the ancient Egyptians. Mayan monumental architecture and magnificently carved stelae and slabs were similar in many respects to those of Ancient Egypt. The Maya constructed elaborate tombs and embalmed their dead as did the Egyptians. The Maya built pyramids.

7

MAYA PYRAMIDS HAD two specialized forms. The first was a twin pyramid complex that consisted of identical flat-topped and stepped pyramids facing each other across a plaza lined by plain stelae and low altar stones. An unroofed enclosure on one side, entered by way of a corbelled arch, contained a carved stele dedicated to the ruler.

The second was the mortuary pyramid of nine stages, symbolizing the nine levels of the underworld. Beneath the pyramid, the tomb of a ruler contained offerings of ceramics, flint, and jade.

All pre-Colombian pyramids were truncated, stepped pyramids and served as the foundations for temples. The largest ones usually sloped less steeply than the Egyptian pyramids, but the smaller ones often had an even steeper incline. Stairways carved into one or more sides of the pyramid led to the temple.

Pyramids were erected not only by the Maya, but by the Toltecs and Aztecs as well. They are found throughout Mexico, Honduras, Guatemala, and El Salvador. The pyramid of El Tajin, in northern Veracruz, features on each of its terraces a series of recessed niches. In the pyramid of the Temple of the Inscriptions at Palenque, a passage beneath the floor of the temple leads to a richly furnished burial crypt deep within the pyramid. One of the largest pyramids in Central America is the Pyramid of the Sun, at Teotihuacan. It is 66 meters (216 feet) high.

The two large adobe pyramids at the coastal site of Moche are traditionally said to be dedicated to the Sun and Moon gods. The stepped terraces of the pyramids reflect the natural terrain of the Andes and the walls of the surrounding buildings were often painted with scenes from mythology.

8

EXCAVATIONS AT THE Olmec site of La Venta indicated that this island had been artificially shaped before any building work began. The structures on the site involved the use of architectural and stone-masonry techniques unheard of in the New World at that time.

The stone itself, which included difficult-to-work basalt, was transported to the site from great distances. A single feature of La Venta—a conical mound—required the importation of more than a million cubic feet of soil. But the most significant aspect of this site is its alignment. At first glance it appeared to have been built on a north-south axis, but more careful measurements showed the axis actually runs eight degrees west of true north.

This "mistake," it transpired, was deliberate: the alignment allowed specific astronomical sightings to be made from the conical mound.

As more information emerges about the developed astronomy of the Olmec, the same deduction must be made as has been made concerning Egypt. A developed astronomy requires a lengthy period of observation. One expert, Dr. M. Popenoe-Hatch, estimates from the internal evidence of their astronomical records that the Olmec must have been on the scene at least as early as 2000 BC.[1] Their actual appearance may have been far earlier still. Their calendar begins in the year 3113 BC, about the time King Menes was engaged in unifying Upper and Lower Egypt.

9

THE OLMEC WERE as dedicated to monumental feats of engineering as their Egyptian counterparts. At San Lorenzo they left a man-made platform one square mile in area, raised 185 feet above ground level. One trench at La Venta yielded up a number of superbly crafted and polished concave mirrors of hematite and magnetite. A stela from the site features a relief that shows one of the mirrors in use. It is attached to a miner's helmet.

The unlikelihood of Olmec deep mining (at a time

---

[1] In *Papers on Olmec and Maya Archaeology*, University of California.

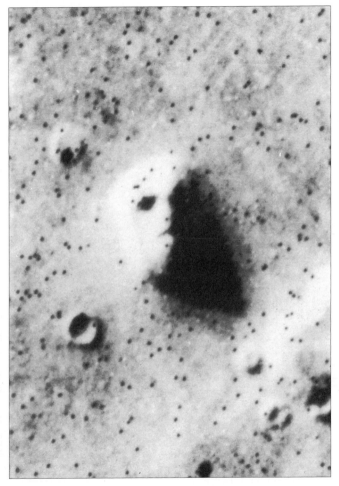

The original *Viking I* space probe photograph of the "Face on Mars," taken in 1976. Surveyor pictures of the same site taken in April 1989 showed nothing like the same detail, but failed to halt speculation about the possibility of an ancient Martian civilization.

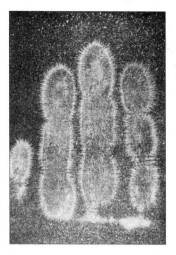

A Kirlian photograph showing the energy field associated with the fingers of a human hand. The Ancient Egyptians appear to have anticipated the discovery (in 1939) of this energy by several thousand years.

South American pyramids, like this one in Mexico, are just one of the many pointers to a prehistoric link with Ancient Egypt.

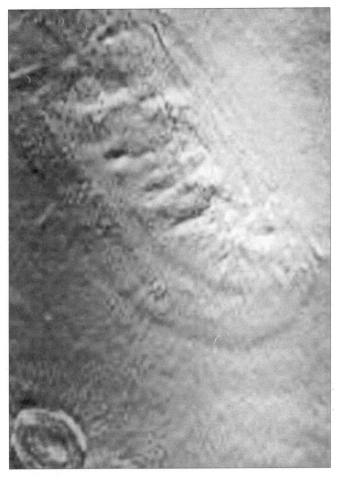

Now you see it, now you don't. NASA re-photographed Cydonia in
1998 and early releases of the pictures showed no sign of the famous
Face. But with the issue of enhanced versions, a hint of features
begins to emerge and the controversy continues.

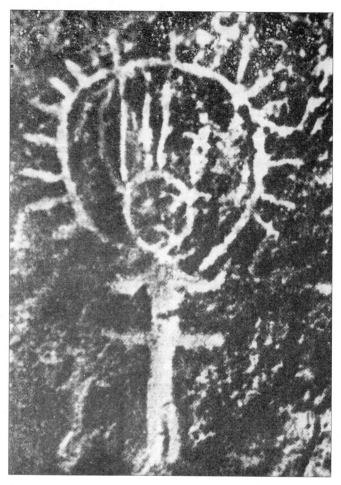

Rock paintings like this one lend credence to the theory of extra-terrestrial visitors to prehistoric Earth. Since scientists insist such visitors could not have originated beyond the solar system, is there a possibility they came down from Mars?

Several more or less fanciful modern maps have shown an "Atlantean" continent during the Ice Age, but it was only through an analysis of ancient maps that the American professor Charles Hapgood was able to show there might be a reality behind the legends of a lost civilization.

The now famous "Baghdad Battery" suggests a knowledge of electricity in the ancient world predating Volta's invention of 1800.

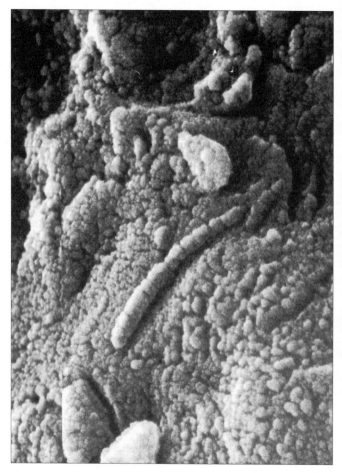

NASA scientists claim these microscopic structures in a Martian meteorite are fossil bacteria, indicative of ancient life on Mars.

Weathering patterns on the Great Sphinx at Giza suggest that it—and therefore the Egyptian civilization itself—is older by several millennia than orthodox Egyptology allows.

Computer enhancement of the "Face on Mars" produced telling detail, like an eye pupil and teeth, not apparent in the original. It was the emergence of such detail that encouraged experts to examine the whole of the Cydonia site.

The "Venus of Willendorf," discovered in 1908 and dated to c. 30,000 BC, was one of the earliest indications that our prehistoric ancestors believed God was a woman.

when archaeologists believe the only metal used in Mesoamerica was gold) has diverted expert attention from the puzzle of why such a mirror should be attached to a helmet in the first place. There may be a clue in an Olmec carving from Tres Zapotes. It shows three figures in an underground passage or cavern. One of them is carrying what appears to be an electrical light source. This is not the only Olmec carving to hint at a high technology in the distant past. A site in the Oaxaca Valley has yielded a relief of an artisan who seems to be carving stone by means of a flame gun. A stela from Chalcatzingo depicts a woman (with curiously European features) apparently operating industrial machinery.

The actual content of ancient carvings is a matter of interpretation. But there is no room for doubt about the engineering skills vested in the site Thor Heyerdahl, referred to as "the mightiest ruins in South America"—the mysterious city of Tiahuanaco.

10

TIAHUANACO LIES NEAR the eastern margin of Lake Titicaca on the Bolivian altiplano. The area is the focus of a great many native legends. The Inca capital Cuzco, for example, was supposed to have been established by the semi-mythic Children of the Sun who had been created and educated at Titicaca. The legendary founder of the Inca royal line, Manco Capac, was believed to be a son of the Sun. He was given a golden wand with which to find his way and emerged from a subterranean passageway to discover he was at Lake Titicaca. The lake was also believed to have been the home of the Creator of All, Viracocha, who lived at Tiahuanaco.

The group of Spanish conquistadors who first stumbled on the ruins faced large open spaces bounded by vertical stone walls, some carved as huge single pieces with sharp right angles. A high pyramidal mound stood opposite a semisubterranean depression, the spaces punctuated by standing human figures cut in single square-sectioned blocks of stone incised with delicate patterns.

There were several freestanding gateways. A large, low enclosed platform is the site of one of the finest of these, the Gate of the Sun. On it, carved reliefs of a frontal figure stand on a stepped mountain and hold serpent staffs. He wears a sunburst headdress and around him winged human and bird-headed figures kneel on one leg. Beneath him are twelve severed heads, also with radial headdresses, linked together by a celestial serpent with multiple heads. At the center of a subterranean temple stood a 22-foot-high stele that showed a figure in a headdress carrying a large beaker in one hand and a strombus shell in the other.

More recent visits by archaeologists have defined six architectural complexes, all probably used for religious ceremonies. The most important structure, the Kala-sasaya platform on which the Gate of the Sun stands, is near the center of the site. The subterranean temple lies to the east, and the enclosures of Putuni, Laka Kollu, and Q'eri Kala are on the west.

Still further west, near the lake, is a sizable ceme-tery. Recent evidence suggests that the site may have been much larger than the part that remains visible to-day and thus have had a sizable resident population.

Experts tell us confidently that Tiahuanaco was oc-cupied from about AD 100 to perhaps AD 1000, but stop short of telling us when it was built.

11

ALAN LANDSBURG, WHO visited the site in the early 1970s, wrote the following description of what he saw:

The walls were put together from megaliths—titanic many-sided stones, accurately cut and ground to a smooth finish, then fitted so precisely that no mortar is needed to bind them. There are no chinks in the walls. I couldn't even pound a chisel between the rocks.

I measured a medium-sized block. It was twenty feet by ten by three. This figured out at around fifty tons . . . for it was hard Andean granite like most of the blocks . . . Each block in these walls is notched so that it interlocks tightly with the stone underneath it, as well as with its neighbors on each side.[2]

One problem, as Landsburg pointed out, was how these structures were built. Tiahuanaco stands at an altitude of 13,125 feet above sea level. While some of the blocks used were of local sandstone, most of them are andesite, the hardest material available in the region. The andesite quarries are some 50 miles away (as the crow flies) on the slopes of the extinct volcano, Kayappia. Landsburg's estimate of fifty tons is, if anything, conservative. Worked blocks weighing up to sixty-five tons have been found. How they were worked is difficult to say. Modern steel tools blunt quickly on this type of rock. Copper was definitely in use in ancient Mesoamerica, but copper tools would be far too soft to do the job.[3]

Some commentators have suggested the use of bronze, although this would require a technology suffi-

---

[2] Quoted from *In Search of Ancient Mysteries* by A. & S. Landsburg, Corgi Books, 1974.

[3] Or perhaps not. The same problem arises with the diorite statues of Kephren in Egypt. While I was in Aswan, a local historian mentioned that in ancient times old tools were much favored over new ones, the reason being that they hardened with use.

ciently advanced to extract tin from the raw ore. There is evidence of prehistoric tin workings in the Cordilleras, some 90 miles from Tiahuanaco. These have not been accurately dated, but appear to be far older than the earliest assigned dates for Tiahuanaco. They had lain hidden for millennia beneath a glacier that only retreated in the 1940s.

If bronze tools *were* used, they must have been made from bronze hardened in some way no longer known to us—and unknown to either Incas or Olmecs to judge from the artifacts that have survived from these cultures. Since there are no chisel marks on the stones, it may be that the builders of Tiahuanaco used some other method entirely. If so, this technology too has been lost to us.

Transportation of the blocks presents another mystery. The horse was only introduced into South America with the coming of the Spaniards. The wheel, while not quite unknown, was used only on toys. So these massive blocks seem to have been dragged by human muscle over a distance in excess of 50 miles to a height in excess of 13,000 feet. Even the local sandstone was not all that local. It was quarried on the western shore of the lake, about ten miles from the site, and broken portions of gigantic blocks weigh up to 100 tons. The assumption is that the original unbroken blocks must have weighed anything up to 400 tons. These too were apparently manhandled to a site a mile southwest of the principal ruins.

12

IF THE SHAPING and transportation of the blocks involved techniques, tools, or equipment now unknown, the building of the city presents even more serious problems for the archaeologist. The notches in the blocks mentioned by Landsburg enable them to be set together in a three-dimensional jigsaw puzzle with each unit interlocking with those above, below, and beside it, like Lego bricks. The result is a construction of exceptional stability, perhaps designed to withstand earthquakes.

But while Lego bricks are child's play to use, Lego bricks weighing between 50 and 400 tons present engineering problems we could solve today only through the use of heavy machinery. What solution did the builders of Tiahuanaco find? It is difficult to imagine teams of workmen on this site whatever techniques were used. The thin mountain air makes exertion difficult and the whole region is so barren, one wonders how they might have been fed.

13

TIAHUANACO IS A port. Its designers incorporated harbors, quays, and docks in its construction. This port is 13,000 feet above sea level and miles from the nearest water.

15 | SHAPING THE STONES

THE BOLIVIAN ALTIPLANO on which Tiahuanaco was built is the most elevated lacustrine basin in the world. Its average height above sea level is 12,300 feet. Tiahuanaco, as we have already seen, is built on an area of the Altiplano that stands almost a thousand feet higher.

There are three lakes on the Altiplano—Titicaca (110 by 35 miles), Poöpo (50 by 20 miles), and Coipasa (20 by 10 miles). All three contain salt water. The area is also noted for its salt marshes, and dry salt beds so extensive they are classified as salt deserts. The lakes are linked. Water from the extensive Titicaca, which is almost 900 feet deep in parts, flows along the sluggish River Desaguadero for some 180 miles before entering Poöpo. From this lake there is a seasonal seepage westward for 65 miles along the Lacahahuira marshland river into the shallow Coipasa. Lake Coipasa has no outlet. Here the waters of the three-lake system either sink into the ground or evaporate. Overall, it is a closed system, fed only by rainfall, that has achieved a state of balance.

The question is, given a wholly freshwater intake through rainfall, how have the lakes remained so salty?

There is a problem with the salt flats themselves. A 50- by 35-mile salt desert lies just south of Lake Coipasa, representing a vast area of the lake that has now completely dried up. Go further south and you reach the Uyuni salt plain, an area of some 80 by 70 miles. To the southwest of this runs a 100-mile-long valley that encloses a chain of very much smaller salt, saltpeter, and borax lakes and ponds. Groundwater feeding into Lake Titicaca passes over crystalline and volcanic rock structures that do not yield salt. Where, then, did so much salt come from? One answer seems to be that it came from the sea.

2

THE ODDEST GEOLOGICAL curiosity of the Andes is a 300-mile-long layer of whitish material at a height of more than 11,500 feet. Scientific examination has indicated this layer is a littoral composed of calcified remains of marine plants. At some stage in the distant past, these great mountains pushed up out of an ocean.

One of the earliest scientists to confirm this unexpected finding was Baron Friedrich von Humboldt, a German botanist and geologist, who made fundamental contributions to scientific knowledge in many areas, including geography, geomorphology, climatology, astronomy, and botany. In 1799, von Humboldt and the French botanist Aimé Bonpland sailed to Spanish colonial lands in South America. During their expedition, which lasted until 1804, they traveled through every type of region in present-day Colombia, Ecuador, Mexico, and Peru. They gathered an enormous amount of data on flora, fauna, climate, astronomy, geology, and the Earth's geomagnetic field. Among the areas investigated was the so-called Giant's Field near Bogotá. This is a rocky plateau 6,500 feet above sea level that derives its name from the vast numbers of enormous fossil bones found there. Von Humboldt quickly discovered that many were those of the mastodon, an elephant-like creature that became extinct with the ending of the last Ice Age.

Like elephants, mastodons required vast quantities of vegetation for food and could not have existed on a high, barren plateau. Their natural habitat is coastal marsh. The discovery of mastodon bones in the Giant's Field suggests that some time prior to 8000 BC (and ranging back 26 million years, the period during which mastodons were widespread) this area was at sea level.

The Andean littoral of calcified marine plants shows two distinct levels of seawater in the Lake Titicaca region, both of them above the level of the lake itself. The higher of these indicates that at one time the whole of the Altiplano was under water, drowned by an inland sea stretching more than 450 miles. The lower of the strandlines marks the boundaries of what geologists refer to as Lake Minchin, after the geographer J. B. Minchin who first noticed the calcareous deposits. This lake, now long disappeared, was substantially larger than the present lakes, but did not flood the Altiplano completely.

What emerges from these findings is a picture of the Altiplano rising from the seabed in remote antiquity and gradually draining to its present, relatively stable, hydrography.

The building of Tiahuanaco, when the Altiplano was at or only a little above sea level, would make far more sense than it does today. It would have permitted the city to function as a port. It would have made the transportation of stones and the work of erection far easier. And it would have provided a hinterland and climate conducive to fertility, thus solving the problem of how the workers were fed.

But if Tiahuanaco really was built during this intermediate period, the evidence of the Giant's Field fossils shows we must be looking at a time period prior to the extinction of the mastodons. And that, in turn, would push this sophisticated city into the depths of the Pliocene.

3

How OLD IS Tiahuanaco likely to be? One expert who worked hard to discover the answer was Arthur Posnansky, whose findings, presented over the thirty-year period between 1914 and 1944, were accepted and endorsed by the Bolivian government. In the multiple volumes of his *Una Metropoli Prehistorica en la America del Sud* and *Tihuanacu—Cuna del Hombre de Las Americas*, Posnansky argued for a phased building of Tiahuanaco, with the first phase carried out at a time when Titicaca was some 100 feet higher than it is today.

Like others who have worked on the site, Posnansky concluded that decorative motifs on the Gate of the Sun actually represented an ancient calendar. Abstract symbols representing sun, moon, planets and even comets, were creatively combined to make up an image of the deity Viracocha. It seems the builders of Tiahuanaco, like the Ancient Egyptians, believed planetary movements gave them insights into the activities of the gods.

There is no doubt at all that the ancient builders had a substantial knowledge of astronomy. Just east of the Gate of the Sun, Posnansky investigated an extensive structure known as the Kalasasaya. The term means "standing pillars"—which is all that is now left of what was once a much more extensive edifice. They proved to be enough, for Posnansky discovered that stones along the east-west axis of the Kalasasaya had been specially carved to enable astronomical observations.

Architectural reconstruction of the Kalasasaya, based on careful measurements taken at the site, suggest the original structure was a hollow step pyramid—that is to say, stepped pyramidal-shaped walls surrounding an open courtyard. This would allow for two sets of observation points on the western terraces.

When Posnansky used the marker stones to make measurements between two solstice points, he found a value of 23° 8′ 48″ for the obliquity of the ecliptic. This deviated from the current value of the obliquity by a small, but significant, amount (3′ 8″). It forced Posnansky to conclude the Kalasasaya had been laid out as an observatory around 15,000 BC.

L

ALTHOUGH POSNANSKY'S BELIEF that the Kalasasaya really *was* an observatory has now been widely accepted, his dating was far more difficult to accept. Nonetheless, the German Astronomical Commission was sufficiently intrigued to send an expedition to Peru and Bolivia in 1926 to check it out.

The expedition included several of the most respected German astronomers of the day. Their work, over a period of almost two years, confirmed Posnansky's suspicions that the Kalasasaya had been used as an observatory. Their preliminary conclusions also supported Posnansky's 15,000 BC date of origin, with the important caveat that the evidence might also point to a date around 9300 BC.

Dr. Rolf Müller, one of the astronomers with the expedition, carried out further work with Posnansky that suggested a possible alternative figure for the obliquity of the ecliptic, yielding two possible dates of 10,000 BC and 4000 BC. Posnansky himself subsequently went on record as accepting a slight modification of Müller's figures, which would leave a choice of 10,150 BC and 4050 BC.[1]

Of the various possible alternatives, all but the most recent figures would place the building of Tiahuanaco in the depths of the Ice Age, exactly as the geological and fossil evidence suggests.

---

[1] At the Twenty-Third International Congress of Americanists.

Whether Tiahuanaco was built in 15,000 BC or AD 800 (as some archaeologists have inferred from pottery fragments), we still have the problem of how. One Indian legend claims the juice of a plant softened the stones enough for them to fit together. It's as good a theory as any, for we have no idea at all of how the stones were worked, or what engineering principles were used to raise them. They represent yet another example of an ancient technology now lost to us.

5

INDICATIONS OF THIS same technology are seen much further afield in South America than Tiahuanaco. Paved roads spanned vast tracts of countryside, extensive terracing and irrigation systems were developed, and enormous, thick walls were constructed of perfectly fitted stones. These engineering works are generally credited to the Incas, but there are strong indications that the attribution is correct only in some instances. The most impressive structures almost certainly were the work of an earlier culture. This even holds good for the Inca's main city, Cuzco.

6

CUZCO, IN SOUTHERN PERU, was the capital of the Inca empire from the fourteenth century until the Spanish conquest. It is situated at an altitude of 3,416 meters (11,207 feet) in a broad Andean valley subject to earthquakes. Inca tribes are believed to have come to Cuzco from the Lake Titicaca region in about the eleventh century while the city was supposed to have been founded by the legendary Manco Capac, first of the Inca rulers.

The name Cuzco means "navel." The city was considered the center of the Inca world. It was certainly the hub from which the Inca road network radiated. Cuzco does not exhibit the organic growth of European cities. It was carefully planned before it was built. Unlike modern preplanned North American cities which tend to be laid out to a grid, Cuzco was designed in the form of a stylized puma. The Huatanay and Tullumayo rivers were straightened to form its tail.

The city is specifically known for examples of an architecture which used enormous cut-stone blocks, so perfectly laid that no mortar was needed. The fortress of Sacsahuaman, which overlooks Cuzco from a hill northwest of the capital, is an outstanding example of this type of construction. It consists of a series of zigzag retaining walls composed of huge stones, each weighing several tons. The walls form three terraces of ramparts. Overlooking them from near the top of the hill is a circular structure divided into small compartments and containing complex ductwork through which water once flowed. Conventional wisdom holds it was built by the Incas in the fifteenth century. Construction is attributed to the ruler Pachacuti, sometime between 1440 and 1470. But most experts agree it is too large to have been completed during a single reign. Some believe the Incas simply added to an already existing site, and the megalithic structures of Sacsahuaman, like the Temple of the Sun in Cuzco, were the work of an earlier culture. They point to the fact that in Sacsahuaman, as in Cuzco, there are examples of two distinct architectural styles—the astounding megalithic structures and the much less impressive Inca buildings made with smaller stones and using mortar.

7

THE SAME PATTERN can be seen at the renowned "lost city" of Machu Picchu, situated about 80 kilometers (50 miles) northwest of Cuzco, overlooking the Urubamba Valley. Its spectacular setting on a high precipice 7,875 feet above sea level between steep mountain peaks has made it one of the most famous archaeological monuments in the world.

The discovery of Machu Picchu came about by accident. In 1536 the defeated Inca ruler fled Cuzco ahead of the Spaniards to found a secret city named Vilcabamba, at which the dynasty managed to survive for a further thirty-six years.

In 1911, the American explorer, historian, and statesman Hiram Bingham led the first of the Yale University Peruvian Expeditions, co-sponsored by the National Geographic Society. One of his main interests was to locate lost Vilcabamba. A peasant offered to guide him to some interesting ruins at the top of a mountain he called Machu Picchu (the "old peak"). Bingham's party hacked their way through dense jungle and made a strenuous, dangerous climb to the site. They reached a massive stone wall by the remains of a temple that took Bingham's breath away. "Dimly, I began to realize that this wall with its adjoining semicircular temple over the cave were as fine as the finest stonework in the world," he wrote later of the find.

Bingham was convinced he had found Vilcabamba, but Spanish documents that came to light later show he was mistaken. This is an important point, for Vilcabamba was definitely constructed by the Incas while there is considerable doubt about who built Machu Picchu.[2] Indeed, the actual function of Machu Picchu is not really understood. It was unknown to the Spanish so their records are of no help, although its architecture suggests a strong emphasis on religion.

That architecture combines fine stone buildings with extensive agricultural terraces, creating the appearance of a settlement literally carved out of the mountainsides. Except that we can be sure it was never used as a settlement. Rather, it was a sacred site, a complex of

---

[2] The city was eventually named after the peak.

temples, palaces, and astronomical observation posts. A few priests and nobles may have lived here, but the bulk of the common people were housed in hamlets well outside the city.

As in other areas of the Inca empire, Machu Picchu exhibits a mix of architectural styles. Some buildings are made from small stones held together with mortar, others comprise courses of dressed stone, while the most impressive structures feature the type of great notched stones found at Tiahuanaco. These are so finely worked and placed that a knife blade cannot be slipped between them. There is no evidence at all that the Incas had the technology to move stones of this size and some evidence that they didn't.

The Incas made their last stand against the Spanish at the promontory of Sacsahuaman. The Spanish chronicler Garcilaso de la Vega describes how an Inca master mason decided to use one of the original stones in his own fortifications. The stone he selected, known as the Tired Stone, had been quarried, but abandoned some distance from the fortress. Under the mason's supervision, ropes were attached to the stone and some 20,000 sweating Incas attempted to drag it to the new fortifications. It proved slow going over the rough ground and when they reached a slope they lost control of the stone. It rolled back down the hill, killing thousands of the Indians.

This single incident is enough to cast doubt on the theory that it was the Incas who hauled these great stones miles, then laid them to a tolerance we would have difficulty matching today.

8

DR. ROLF MÜLLER, the astronomer who worked with Posnansky at Tiahuanaco, applied his expertise to the structures at Cuzco and Machu Picchu as well. He reached two conclusions.

The first, based on his investigation of the Temple of the Sun at Cuzco, was that the ancient walls and circular Holy of Holies functioned the same way as the temples of Ancient Egypt aligned to the solstice sunrise.

The second, with even more far-reaching implications, was again based on ecliptic obliquity. Müller's measurements of dressed stone structures at both Cuzco and Machu Picchu convinced him they were aligned to an obliquity of 24°, which meant they were originally set up at least 4,000 years ago.

But it is important to note that this dating, even though it extends orthodox dating for the Inca civilization, is derived from Intermediate Period dressed stone alignments. Müller believed, on the basis of his experience at Tiahuanaco, that the great megaliths were substantially older.

¶

SIXTY MILES NORTHWEST of Cuzco lies the remnants of another structure on a mountain spur above the village of Ollantaytambu. Several hundred rough stone steps join a series of Inca terraces that lead to the fortress ruins now named for their village. There are signs of Inca building, using rough stones and mortar, but beyond and above them lies a massive stone wall that marks the divide with an earlier, more impressive architecture. This early architecture includes six colossal monoliths that stand on the topmost terrace. These monsters, which form a perfect length of wall, vary between eleven and fourteen feet high, three to six feet thick, and an average of six feet wide. Their linkage with Tiahuanaco is established by common symbols carved at both sites.

These huge blocks—and the many others found at Ollantaytambu—were quarried from the mountain at the other side of the valley. Two streams had to be crossed before they could be dragged up the mountainside and erected. Here again, no one knows how this could have been accomplished.

The picture that emerges from all of this is of Mesoamerican engineering standards that peaked in prehistory and gradually degenerated into historical times. Alongside this are hints in ancient carvings of light sources that did not rely on fire, and stone-carving tools that did.

Excavations about a mile southwest of the main Tiahuanaco ruins have unearthed quantities of precision-cut stones that look like dies for the casting of metal machine parts. If these are remnants of an ancient technology carried to Earth by colonizing Martians, they are not the only remnants.

16 | SCIENCE OF THE ANCIENT WORLD

THERE IS LITTLE emotional impact in the realization that the Egyptians used lever technology to build their pyramids. More efficient or not, more economical or not, we still manage to convince ourselves such a system was somehow crude and primitive by comparison with modern mechanical methods. But they may have had electrical technology as well.

Modern use of electricity dates back no further than the nineteenth century. When Luigi Galvani's experiments with "animal electricity" were published in 1791, the Italian physicist Alessandro Volta began experiments that led him to theorize animal tissue was not necessary for conduction of electricity. Proof of the theory was his invention, in 1800, of the so-called voltaic pile, then believed to be the world's first battery. There is, however, evidence of electrical knowledge at a much earlier date.

2

AS EARLY AS 600 BC the Greeks were aware of a peculiar property of amber. When rubbed with a piece of fur, it developed the ability to attract small pieces of material and feathers—an electrical effect (static). The Romans knew of the same effect, but went further in that they protected their important buildings from "Jupiter's bolts" (lightning strike) through the use of metal conductors.

This sort of knowledge does not presuppose real understanding, but a sequence of events that began in 1936 suggests a developed electrical technology in ancient times.

Wilhelm König, the German director of the Iraq Museum laboratory, described a newly discovered find in these words:

> A vase-like vessel of light yellow clay, whose neck had been removed, contained a copper cylinder which was held firmly by asphalt. The vase was about 15 cm high; the sheet copper cylindrical tube with bottom had a diameter of 26 mm and was 9 cm long. In it, held by a kind of stopper of asphalt, was a completely oxidized iron rod, the top of which projected about 1 cm above the stopper and was covered by a yellowish-gray, fully oxidized thin coating of a metal which looked like lead. The bottom end of the iron rod did not extend right to the bottom of the cylinder, on which was a layer of asphalt about 3 mm deep.

When the various parts were brought together and examined, König realized it was only necessary to add acid or alkaline liquid for the device to be transformed into an electrical element. In other words, it was a battery. But it was a battery that had been discovered in a Parthian village, which meant it had been manufactured no later than AD 226 . . . and might have been constructed as long ago as 248 BC. Dr. Arne Eggebrecht duplicated the artifact and added alkaline liquid in the form of grape juice. It generated a measured half volt of electricity.

A Parthian battery c. 248 BC to AD 226 is a long way from Ancient Egypt, but there have been finds that bring it closer.

3

ONE OF THE great mysteries of the ancient world is how gold plating was achieved. In some cases it is obvious that leaves of gold were simply beaten on. In others the bonding is so strong and the plating so thin and smooth that it could only be duplicated today by means of electroplating. One such object, in Eggebrecht's possession, is an Osiris statue in gold-plated silver. It could have been plated using König's battery in less than three hours. The statue has been dated to about 400 BC.

By the time we reach back to the remote antiquity of the Old Kingdom, this sort of hard evidence disappears, but inferences of an electrical technology remain surprisingly strong. One negative inference is the lack of smoke stains in the earliest of Egyptian tombs and other structures such as the pyramids. In constructing these edifices, the builders needed light, and torches leave a smoke stain. The absence of such stains suggests a smokeless light source. Such a light source exists in the form of sesame-oil lamps, the usual explanation put forward by modern Egyptologists. But the alternative possibility that the source may have been electrical is suggested by some curious phenomena associated with the Great Pyramid.

4

ARAB LEGEND HELD for centuries that the pyramid was haunted. A vampiric shade flitted through its inner galleries and mysterious lights sometimes appeared at its apex. Scientists dismiss the vampire, but the mysterious lights are real enough. They are caused by static electricity that manifests as an aurora in certain climatic conditions.

A curious experience of Sir William Siemens shows

that the pyramid generates static electricity even when an aurora is not present. The Siemens family of engineers, inventors, and industrialists were early pioneers in the field of electricity. In 1847, Werner von Siemens founded a German telegraphic manufacturing and repair business that was to become one of the major electrical manufacturing companies in Europe. His brother, born Carl Wilhelm Siemens, went to England in 1843 and became the head of the English branch of the Siemens firm. He invented and improved a water meter in the 1850s and promoted many of Werner's projects. He Anglicized his name to William and was eventually knighted.

On a trip to Egypt, Sir William visited the Great Pyramid and climbed to its summit with an Arab guide. While they were standing on the topmost course, the guide remarked that when he raised his hand with his fingers spread, it caused an intense ringing noise. Siemens ventured an index finger and felt a prickling sensation. A little later, trying to drink some wine, he felt a distinct shock. At this point his background convinced him he was dealing with some sort of electrical phenomenon and he decided to create a makeshift Leyden jar, an apparatus for the storage of static electricity.

The earliest Leyden jars were glass vials partially filled with water. Their stoppers were pierced with a wire or nail that dipped into the water. Static electricity traveled down the wire. Anybody touching the wire would receive a shock, proving that electricity had been stored. The modern version is coated with metal foil. A brass rod touches the inner cover and extends out of the top of the jar through a rubber stopper.

Siemens converted the wine bottle by wrapping it with a moistened newspaper. It was a crude enough device, but the static charge at the peak of the pyramid was so high that sparks began to stream from the bottle. The guide panicked, accused him of witchcraft, and tried to grab his companion. Siemens knocked the guide unconscious with an electrical jolt from the bottle.

5

IT MAY BE that the static associated with the pyramid is an accidental effect, but it would be unwise to make this an absolute assumption. There are so many indications of high-level scientific knowledge built into the pyramid that almost anything seems possible. It has, for example, been sited so that a meridian drawn through its apex divides the Nile delta exactly in two, while diagonals drawn at right angles neatly enclose it. Shadow patterns from the group of three pyramids at Giza serve as an accurate compass. The Great Pyramid functions as a surveyor's theodolite: once you know its latitude, you can mark survey lines with nothing more complicated than a plumb line. You simply sight on it against the sun. The height of the pyramid in relation to the perimeter of its base incorporates the value *pi* (which is also incorporated in some Egyptian temple doorways). The construction of the base incorporates values for the solar, sidereal, and orbital years.

The list goes on to such an extent that it becomes difficult to take seriously—the reason, presumably, that so many archaeologists refer to those who study such things as "pyramidiots." But however much scholarly scorn is heaped upon it, the fact remains that the values are there, and not all of them can be coincidental.

6

THE GREAT PYRAMID contains one further piece of evidence for a high degree of scientific knowledge that has not been ridiculed by scholars—the sarcophagus in the King's Chamber.

This curious container was cut from a single block of chocolate-colored granite, heavily flecked with feldspar, quartz, and mica particles. It is known to have been hollowed out by drilling, but a puzzled Sir Flinders Petrie calculated that the drill pressure would have had to be in the region of two tons—considerably in excess of anything other than a modern mechanical rig.

If the Ancient Egyptians did not use something like this (and there is not the slightest evidence that they did) they must have developed, or inherited, a technology currently unknown. It enabled them to produce paper-thin stone bowls and cut hieroglyphs into diorite so hard that it would blunt most modern tools.

7

IF THE EGYPTIANS really did have insights into static electrical field phenomena, it did not define the limits of their knowledge. There is evidence they had an understanding of psychotronics.

Psychotronics first came to the attention of Western scientists in the late 1960s with the release of an extraordinary Czech documentary movie. As described by Sheila Ostrander and Lynn Schroeder, who saw the film at a Parapsychology Conference in Moscow:

> The content, for a science film, was . . . dazzling. One after another, the camera lit up what seemed to be modern sculptures—gleaming forms that could have been created by Brancusi, or more intricate ones perhaps by Dali. Other objects looked like precision cut components for machines that hadn't been invented yet, spare parts from 2001. Still other small metal and wood sculptures were reminiscent of these "ritual objects" set out by the museums of the world, from the British Museum in London to the little dusty museums of Asian Turkey and southern Egypt. But these are not sculptures, the objects aren't in a museum. This is an ordinary apartment in a small town in Czechoslovakia. The

devices sitting on the table supposedly collect psychotronic energy given off by living things.[1]

There is much less controversy now about "energy given off by living things" than there was in the 1960s. Since then Dr. Harold Saxon Burr, who was for forty-three years professor of neuroanatomy at Yale University School of Medicine, has been able to measure an electrical field phenomenon generated by the human body—and other living organisms—using a sensitive vacuum tube voltmeter. In women, this field has been found to vary in potential at the point of ovulation. Its fluctuations have also shown promise in the early detection of certain diseases, notably cancer.

The cautious Burr experimented with the field for more than fifty years before announcing his findings in 1972. They confirmed even more spectacular work that had been quietly under way in the then Soviet Union since 1939. In that year, a Russian engineer named Semyon Davidovich Kirlian first experimented with high frequency electrical field generators.

8

KIRLIAN BECAME INTRIGUED by the problem of photographing the sparks he had noticed jumping between high frequency electrodes and the skin of patients under treatment in the hospital. Since he wanted traces of the sparks themselves, he abandoned the idea of an optical camera in favor of placing a photographic plate between the electrode and the skin. He could not use the safer hospital electrodes, which were made from glass, for fear of fogging his plate, so he took his

---

[1] *Psychic Discoveries Behind the Iron Curtain* by Sheila Ostrander and Lynn Schroeder, Bantam Books, New York, 1971.

chances with metal and burned his hand severely in the process.

But he got a picture. It was not the sort of picture he expected. Instead of electrical spark traces, he found he had an image of his hand surrounded by a luminescent nimbus.

Kirlian photography, as the process became known, is now so widespread that Kirlian palm prints are made at public exhibitions. You place your hand on a metal plate, experience a mild tingling, and are presented with the developed print five minutes later. Although the esoteric community likes to claim that Kirlian photography takes pictures of auras, the process is actually more subtle. Kirlian "cameras" generate a high frequency electrical field in the range of 75,000 to 200,000 oscillations per second. What is photographed is the *interaction* between this field and a bioplasmic energy generated, as Burr was to confirm, by living matter.

Psychotronic generators accumulate this energy and put it to work. The film watched by Ostrander and Schroeder showed one such generator attract small items like matches, bits of glass, and even bread as if they were capable of being magnetized. The effect still worked under water, thus ruling out an electrostatic field phenomenon. Another generator proved capable of halting the spin of a needle placed on an electrically driven rotor. Yet another was capable of driving a small blade.

All these were demonstration effects, but the commercial potential of psychotronics may not be far away. Dr. Zdenek Rejdak described one generator capable of driving a small electric motor. After an initial half hour charge, it was capable of running the motor for up to fifty hours on the basis of a few minutes top-up charge each day.

Psychotronics is not confined to mechanical effects. Seeds radiated with psychotronic energy developed into plants twice the size of those grown from a control batch. The energy also proved capable of separating out a pollutant dye dissolved in water.

Psychotronic generators withstood the onslaught of scientists determined to find a less radical explanation of the effects. Following tests carried out at Hradec Králové University, Czech Republic, a spokesman commented: "The experiments have excluded any conceivable physical agent—even heat."

Physicist and mathematician Dr. Julius Krmessky, is on record as saying: "The radiation goes right through glass, water, wood, cardboard, any type of metal . . . and its strength doesn't diminish at all. Furthermore, the mind seems to control this energy."[2]

But if scientists are happy that psychotronic energy exists, some of its effects are very difficult to swallow. For psychotronics has extended into the controversial realm of parapsychology. Czech engineers have created a generator that can score 100 percent in ESP card tests.

9

ALTHOUGH TOO OBSCURE to attract much media attention, psychotronic research has survived the collapse of the Soviet Union and continues, largely in Eastern Europe, to this day.

One thing that emerged even at an early stage was that the essential secret of a psychotronic generator is its form. A combination of the right mix of metals with a specific shape creates the conditions in which psychotronic energy may be accumulated.

The whole of modern psychotronic technology is based on the discoveries of Robert Pavlita, who was

---

[2] Quoted from *Psychic Discoveries Behind the Iron Curtain* by Sheila Ostrander and Lynn Schroeder, Bantam Books, New York, 1971.

design director of a large Czech textile company in the 1960s. He used copper, iron, steel, brass, gold, and even wood to construct his machines. All these materials, with the exception of steel, were used in Ancient Egypt. Nor is this coincidental. Pavlita, a technical genius interested in alternative forms of energy since childhood, is known to have drawn his inspiration from the study of "ancient texts." What these texts were he was not prepared to say, but the movie released by the Czech authorities to demonstrate his work contained artistically intercut scenes of Egypt and one of his generators seems to have been based on the form of the *ankh*, a looped cross that was the Egyptian symbol of life. Another basic form used in his machines was the pyramid.

10

COINCIDENTALLY, ANOTHER CZECH—Karel Drbal, a radio engineer from Prague—had already discovered an intriguing curiosity about the pyramid shape. Tiny models of the Great Pyramid, made from cardboard (later Styrofoam) generated a mysterious energy capable of sharpening razor blades placed beneath them. Whether this energy was psychotronic—that is, drawn from a living source—Drbal did not speculate. But he was able to convince the Czech authorities the energy actually existed. They granted him a patent on his Cheops Pyramid Razor Blade Sharpener in 1959.

11

THE ORIGINAL OF Drbal's model was not bent to the task of ensuring Ancient Egypt remained clean shaven. Rather, it was aligned to the constellation Orion so that the soul of the dead pharaoh might travel accurately and safely to join this heavenly body of stars. The term "soul" is, however, misleading. The

Egyptians actually believed that humanity had three souls. These were known as the *ba*, the *ib*, and the *ka*.

The *ba* was the bird-soul. It was supposed to remain in the individual's tomb, standing guard, so to speak, over his or her embalmed body. A small perch (and sometimes a wooden image) was often provided in the tomb for this purpose. The *ib* was the inner essence of the individual's heart, which was taken to the under-world by the jackal-headed god Anubis, there to be weighed against a feather in the Halls of Judgment. De-scriptions of the *ka* in Egyptian literature have led to speculation that this "soul" may not have been entirely the result of religious belief. It was known as the *double* and thought of as a mirror image of the physical body, but composed of finer matter. Such a description links it with an odd fact of psychological life—out-of-body ex-perience.

12

THE PHENOMENON OF out-of-body experi-ence is well attested. In 1886, three founding fathers of the Society for Psychical Research, Francis Gurney, Frederick Myers, and Frank Podmore, published a com-prehensive tome entitled *Phantasms of the Living* that detailed 350 cases. In 1951, Sylvan Muldoon and Here-ward Carrington added another 100 in their *Phenomena of Astral Projection*. Three years later, Hornell Hart was examining 288 cases in the *Journal of the American Society for Psychical Research*. Another psychical re-searcher, Robert Crockall entered the lists in 1961 and between then and 1978 published no fewer than nine books of case histories. The scientist Celia Green ap-pealed for information on the subject in the late 1960s, and had 326 replies from people with personal experi-ence. John Poynton added 122 more in 1978.

Sylvan Muldoon was among the first to describe in print what out-of-body experience felt like:

I was floating! I was floating in the very air, rigidly horizontal, a few feet above the bed . . . Slowly, still zigzagging with the strong pressure in the back of my head, I was moved toward the ceiling, all the while horizontal and powerless . . .

I managed to turn round. There were two of me! I was beginning to believe myself insane. There was another "me" lying quietly upon the bed! It was difficult to convince myself that this was real, but consciousness would not allow me to doubt what I saw.[3]

James Randi, the arch skeptic of paranormal phenomena, had an out-of-body experience that he subsequently dismissed as an hallucination.

But the point is not the nature of the experience so much as the fact that it occurs. It is easy to see how the Ancient Egyptians could have based their belief in an immortal *ka* on reports like those of Muldoon and Randi, hallucinatory or not.

They were not the only culture to have been impressed by the phenomenon. A survey has shown no fewer than fifty-seven peoples worldwide currently hold a firm belief in some sort of second body—and the list does not pretend to be definitive.

This gives a new perspective on why Khufu elected to have his launch-pad to Orion constructed in the shape of a pyramid.

In view of Robert Pavlita's discovery that it is shape which determines the function of a psychotronic generator and the hints that he drew his inspiration from Ancient Egypt, one must wonder if there is something about the Great Pyramid designed to stimulate out-of-body experience. There is evidence that it might.

---

[3] Quoted from *The Projection of the Astral Body* by Sylvan Muldoon and Hereward Carrington, Rider, London, 1968.

13

DR. PAUL BRUNTON was a well-traveled English author who died in 1981. In the early 1930s, Brunton made a trip to Egypt and contrived to spend a night alone in the King's Chamber of the Great Pyramid. Stretched out on the floor in total darkness he discovered:

> . . . all my muscles became taut, after which a paralyzing lethargy began to creep over my limbs. My entire body became heavy and numb . . . my feet became colder and colder. The feeling developed into a kind of iciness which moved by imperceptible degrees up my legs . . . All sensation in the lower limbs was numbed . . .
>
> When the chill reached my chest . . . the rest of my body was completely paralyzed . . . At last my concentrated consciousness lay in the head alone . . . I had the sensation of being caught up in a tropical whirlwind and seemed to pass upwards through a narrow hole . . . I had gone ghost-like clean out of my earthly body . . .
>
> At first I found myself lying on my back, as horizontal as the body I had just vacated, floating above the stone floor-block . . . I gazed down upon the deserted body of flesh and bone . . . The inexpressive face was upturned, the eyes were scarcely open, yet the pupils gleamed sufficiently to indicate the lids were not really closed . . .
>
> I noted a trail of faint silvery light projecting itself down from me, the new *me*, to the cataleptic creature who lay upon the block.[4]

---

[4] Quoted from *A Search in Secret Egypt* by Dr. Paul Brunton, Samuel Weiser, Inc., U.S., 1988.

Brunton believed he had reached the state of death. But his description, from the initial creeping paralysis to the floating sensation during which he looks down at his physical body, is identical to that given by scores of others who have undergone an out-of-body experience.

17 | THE RESTLESS EARTH

IT IS POSSIBLE that the archaeology of historical Egypt might have unearthed further links to an ancient hi-tech civilization were it not for a development that mirrored, on a smaller scale, the great disaster at the end of the last Ice Age.

Because of the supreme importance of the Nile to the economy of their country, the Egyptians from ancient times measured the level of the river against a marker now known as a Nilometer. The Nilometer at Semneh shows the water level dropped by twenty-two feet in a single year at the end of the Middle Kingdom period. There are only two things that could have caused this effect: a massive loss in river volume or an equally massive drop in the level of the bedrock through which the river flows.

The Nile flood in October was fed by monsoon rainfall on the Ethiopian highlands during the previous April and May. A drought in Ethiopia would obviously influence the river level, but even if no rain fell at all, it would not lower the level by anything remotely approaching twenty-two feet. Thus we are left with a sudden drop in the bedrock, which presupposes seismic activity of almost unimaginable ferocity. Immanuel Velikovsky linked this with the biblical Exodus of the Children of Israel out of Egypt.

Contrary to the doctrine of uniformitarianism, there is evidence that natural disasters *can* influence the course of history—the destruction of Pompeii and Herculaneum are striking examples. Despite this, a majority of scientists continue to dismiss the catastrophe model as relevant only to unimportant aberrations in an otherwise calm, uneventful progression.[1] But for Velikovsky there have been historical periods in which nature was anything but calm. His study of ancient records convinced him that a major series of catastrophes occurred in the second millennium BC, followed by another in the eighth century BC.

Whatever orthodox science may think of Velikovsky's theories on the *cause* of various terrestrial disasters, his historical research has never been faulted. Comparison of the ancient records of many cultures shows there were widespread natural cataclysms, mainly related to tectonic and volcanic activity, over a relatively brief period in the second millennium BC. In Egypt, that period coincided with the downfall of the Middle Kingdom.

2

A RECORD OF the events from a human perspective is contained in the *Leiden Papyrus* 344, a work written by the scribe Ipuwer who appears to have had the misfortune of living through them. The eyewitness describes "years of noise" during which towns were destroyed, residences overturned in the space of a minute and the Nile actually ran dry in Upper Egypt. "All is ruin," wrote Ipuwer. "The land turns round as does a potter's wheel."

This is a vivid portrayal of massive, prolonged tectonic activity and the devastation it caused. Ipuwer goes on to tell how ships were cast adrift and many were sucked into whirlpools formed by submarine earth

---

[1] There are recent (1994) indications that this viewpoint may be changing as scientists face growing evidence that large-scale meteor impacts on our planet are far more common than was previously believed.

movements. Rivers became polluted and undrinkable, freak weather destroyed crops, volcanic fire erupted from the cracked earth to consume gates, columns, and walls. With the physical foundation of the culture crumbling, plague broke out. "Blood," bewailed Ipuwer, "is everywhere."

3

DRAWING ON THIS papyrus and two other sources, Velikovsky constructed a picture of the time that contained parallel after parallel (some in identical words) with the description given in the Old Testament of environmental conditions at the time of the Exodus. The similarities eventually convinced him that the ancient Hebrew and Egyptian records were describing the same event.

There was a serious problem with this theory. Scholarly opinion had long identified Rameses II as the pharaoh of the Oppression, which left his successor, Merneptah, the likeliest candidate as pharaoh of the Exodus. But these were Nineteenth Dynasty kings, which would place the Exodus around 1220 BC and not at the end of the Middle Kingdom, almost 600 years earlier.

At the same time there were historical problems with assigning Merneptah as pharaoh of the Exodus in that the king's stele refers to Israel firmly resident in Palestine during his reign, not wandering the desert in search of the Promised Land.

In order to resolve these difficulties, Velikovsky made an extensive comparison between the histories of Israel and Egypt over a prolonged period. It led him to conclude traditional dating was out of sync throughout, again by some 600 years. The evidence for this startling discovery was published in 1953 in a volume entitled *Ages in Chaos* which, unlike *Worlds in Collision*, has never been seriously questioned by scholars, although it has never been accepted either.

L

       IF VELIKOVSKY was correct in his revision of historical dating, and the events described by Ipuwer were, in fact, the events of the biblical Exodus, then it becomes possible to make a fuller reconstruction of what happened by combining both Hebrew and Egyptian sources.

At the time, somewhere around 1786 BC, the Twelfth Dynasty Queen Sobekneferure occupied the Egyptian throne. The country had been reunified by Mentuhotep a little more than half a century previously. While pyramid building had died out, there are numerous pointers to a rich, secure, and flourishing culture. The Hawara labyrinth was still relatively new, as was the Chapel of Senusret at Karnak. Large fortresses had been established between the First and Second Cataracts in Nubia.

It was against this background that the seismic upheavals began. Velikovsky had a talent for describing cataclysm and I can do no better than to quote him here. He begins by considering the possibility that Mount Sinai was an active volcano, then goes on:

> Volcanic activity spread far and wide, Mount Sinai was but one furnace in a great plain of smoking furnaces.

> Earth, sea and sky participated in the upheaval. The sea overflowed the land, lava gushed out of the riven ground . . . In a great geologic catastrophe the bottom of the sea fell and the waters rushed into the chasms. The earth trembled, the volcanoes threw smoke and fire out of the interior of the earth, cliffs were torn away, molten rock ran along the valleys, the dry earth became sea, the bowels of the mountains groaned and the skies thundered unceasingly . . .

The experience, according to the Scriptures, was so majestic and terrible that even after a long line of succeeding generations it could not be forgotten.[2]

The most immediate result of this tectonic activity was river pollution. Both the Leiden Papyrus and the Book of Exodus state categorically that rivers "turned to blood," which suggests an upsurge of red clay. Fish died in large numbers and their decomposition added to the pollution. Soon the water was utterly undrinkable: the Egyptians dug near the river in the hope of discovering fresh supplies. It seems they did not succeed. In the Leiden Papyrus, Ipuwer laments:

That is our water! That is our happiness! What shall we do in respect thereof? All is ruin![3]

What appear to be constant earthquakes quickly brought down buildings. An Egyptian source claims all the mud-brick houses of Egypt were demolished, as were many of the more solidly constructed stone-built temples. Freak weather conditions accompanied the seismic activity, notably in the form of hailstorms. These flattened growing grain crops, destroyed fruit and, in many instances, uprooted trees. Sometimes the storms were accompanied by coincident volcanic activity that added the destructive element of fire to the destructive winds and hail. Seen from the religious perspective of the Hebrews:

. . . the Lord sent thunder and hail, and the fire ran along upon the ground; and the Lord rained hail upon the land of Egypt.

---

[2] *Ages in Chaos*, Sphere Books, London, 1973.
[3] *Ibid.*

So there was hail, and fire mingled with the hail, very grievous, such as there was none like it in all the land of Egypt since it became a nation.[4]

The conditions obviously affected the country's livestock. The Leiden Papyrus states:

Behold, cattle are left to stray and there is none to gather them together. Each man fetches for himself those that are branded in his name . . . All animals, their hearts weep. Cattle moan . . .

With their crops and homes destroyed, their animal husbandry in chaos, the Egyptians quickly fell prey to hunger and disease. But worse was to come. Both the Old Testament and the Leiden Papyrus mention perpetual darkness across Egypt, presumably occasioned by the dust clouds and fumes thrown up by the protracted seismic activity. This sometimes grew so dense that, according to the eyewitness accounts, people were unable to see more than a few feet in front of them. Needless to say, many deaths followed. Velikovsky quotes Artapanus, another ancient source:

Hail and earthquake by night so that those who fled from the earthquake were killed by the hail and those who sought shelter from the hail were destroyed by the earthquake . . .

Those with no ties to property—the slaves and poor of Egypt—fled into the desert regions where, possibly, the seismic activity was a little less severe. Their ruined country, desolate, barren and helpless, fell, within weeks, to the vicious multitudes of Amalek, now more usually known as the Hyksos. History records that the invaders did not have to fight a single battle.

---

[4] Exod. 9:23–24.

Whether or not one accepts Velikovsky's theory of an extraordinary period of destructive seismic activity, the historical fact remains that the cultural and architectural peaks achieved during the Middle Kingdom were never recovered.

The Asiatic Hyksos ruled Egypt for just over a century, but even after the establishment of the New Kingdom, around 1567 BC, Egypt never regained her former glory. The ancient science and technology inherited from the depths of prehistory all but collapsed. But at least one aspect of it was preserved by a priest who fled the devastation along with the poor and the slaves. His name was Moses.

THE OLD TESTAMENT books of Exodus, Leviticus, Numbers, and Deuteronomy are the only available sources of Moses' life. No contemporary Egyptian documents mention him, and later traditions recorded by Philo of Alexandria, Josephus, and various rabbinical writings are elaborations of the biblical story, rather than fresh sources of information.

The biblical story itself is drawn from a variety of sources, the earliest of which postdates Moses by more than 200 years. There are signs that the basic facts have been elaborated to create a mythic figure.

The story of how baby Moses was cast on the Nile and found in the rushes is well known. It is not so widely realized that the same story was told about Sargon, king of Akkad, who lived about 2350 BC, more than 1,000 years before the time of Moses, and even about the god Horus in Egyptian mythology. Despite this, the broad outlines of Moses' story seem reasonable enough. According to the biblical account, he grew up at Pharaoh's court. The Old Testament claims he was discovered as a baby by Pharaoh's daughter, who decided to raise him as her own. Scholars suggest a more likely explanation might be found in the Egyptian practice of taking hostages from their Semitic vassals, giving them Egyptian training, and sending them back to lead their people with an ingrained Egyptian viewpoint.

Whatever the reason, Moses' position at court would have ensured admission into the initiate priesthood. A New Testament reference suggests he "was learned in all the wisdom of the Egyptians, and was mighty in words and in deeds."[1] Philo of Alexandria enlarges on this considerably. He states that Moses learned mathematics, geometry, harmonics, poetry, philosophy, Egyptian and Assyrian script, and astronomy. Almost any one of these is enough to show he had joined the closed elite of the priesthood. Sir E. A. Wallis Budge, a former keeper of Egyptian Antiquities at the British Museum, suggested he might even have risen to the rank of High Priest. If this is correct, it would have given him access to every branch of specialist historical, religious, and scientific knowledge vested in the temples. If the training was really meant to give Moses some Egyptian sympathies, the ploy did not work. According to the Old Testament he was forced to flee to Midian after killing an Egyptian who struck an Israelite. In exile he married the daughter of the high priest of Midian—another indication of where he stood. It was also during his exile that he had what might be termed a visionary experience. God spoke to him at a burning bush and instructed him to lead the Hebrew captives out of Egypt. At this point, the biblical account, with its religious overtones, dovetails abruptly with Velikovsky's secular research.

2

IT IS OBVIOUS from both the Hebrew and Egyptian records (assuming Velikovsky was correct in his revision of historical dating) that a series of spectacular disasters befell the Egyptian nation. The Hebrews—and quite possibly the Egyptians themselves—believed these disasters were the result of divine intervention. This raises the question of whether Moses believed it.

---

[1] Acts 7:22.

As an initiate, his scientific knowledge might have given him insights into the natural causes of seismic activity. But this is by no means certain. At this comparatively late date in Egyptian history, much of the knowledge carried over from the prehistoric proto-civilization may have been lost. If not, there is still the question of viewpoint. The movement of the stars, well observed and understood, was nonetheless considered by the Egyptians to be the physical activity of their gods. It is possible that tectonic activity, perhaps equally well understood, might be seen as the anger of the gods.

Yet there has to remain a third possibility—that Moses was a cynical opportunist, seizing on natural phenomena to bolster a political position. There is an intriguing corollary to this third possibility. Moses' understanding of seismic activity could have been drawn only from his training in the Egyptian priesthood. But his knowledge would have been shared by the other priests. When Moses claimed his "Lord" was causing the plagues and the earthquakes, his lay followers may have accepted it, but the loyal priesthood would have advised Pharaoh the Lord was doing nothing of the sort. Despite the earthquakes, Pharaoh would then have refused Moses' demand to release the Israelite slaves. Interestingly, this is exactly what the Old Testament says happened. Time and again, "the Lord hardened Pharaoh's heart" just when it seemed Moses might get his way.

But if the Lord really was involved, it is difficult to see why He would aid Moses to bully Pharaoh, then support Pharaoh in his determination to resist. It seems much more likely it was the priesthood who stiffened Pharaoh's resolve by assuring him the "miracles" were far from miraculous.

But Pharaoh *did* release the Israelites eventually, perhaps because his position simply became untenable. If the disasters that befell his country were even half as bad as the contemporary descriptions, then he had enough on his plate without having to worry about imminent rebellion. As conditions worsened to the point of cultural collapse, he may have decided to solve one of his many problems by the expedient of giving in. Having given in, however, he changed his mind again and pursued the fugitives.[2] Moses parted the Red Sea, permitting his people to cross, but when Pharaoh's army tried to follow, "the waters returned, and covered the chariots, and the horsemen, and all the host of Pharaoh that came into the sea after them; there remained not so much as one of them."[3]

Ǝ

VELIKOVSKY TAKES THE parting of the Red Sea literally and explains it as the action of a fierce storm on the waters. Since no such phenomena has ever been witnessed in modern times, even during tornadoes and hurricanes, it is difficult to envisage a wind strong enough to part the sea while still allowing anyone to move.

In fact, this aspect of the Old Testament story may well be a mythic accretion that simply reinforces Moses' links with the initiate priesthood. A very similar miracle was attributed to the Fourth Dynasty priest Tchatcha-em-ankh. I drew largely on sources quoted by Wallis Budge to piece together the original tale in an unpublished work about Nectanebus II, the last native Egyptian pharaoh:

There is a story told of ancient days when the Pharaoh Snefru ruled. It appears this king, who was father to Khufu whom the Greeks call Cheops, was

---

[2] Or possibly *her* mind if Velikovsky is correct, for his dating would make Queen Sobekneferure a candidate as Pharaoh of the Exodus along with Senusret.

[3] Exod. 14:28.

subject to fugue. On a day in summer, falling into low spirits, he called on his Court to find some means whereby his heart might be lightened.

Failing in the more usual remedies of song and gossip, the nobles called on the assistance of the wisest man in Egypt of that day, a priest and writer of books, one Tchatcha-em-ankh. The priest advised the king thus:

"Go, Majesty, to the lake near the palace and there sail upon it in the boat which I have had prepared for thee."

So the king went to the great ornamental lake where the ibis waded in the shallows and there discovered a craft unlike any other, graven with the forms of fabulous beasts and leafed with beaten gold. The paddles of this craft were of ebony, inlaid with gold and in place of oarsmen were twenty female virgins, the most delicately beautiful in all of Egypt. Tchatcha-em-ankh had caused these young women to be dressed in netting, like that of sea fishermen, so that the most intimate aspects of their bodies were at once concealed and revealed.

When the king entered the boat, these nubile women manned the oars and sang sweetly to him while they rowed him hither and thither. And Seneferu, watching the fluid movement of their bodies beneath the netting, became aroused; and with arousal, his heart too rose up . . .

It seems that the leader of the nubile group, unaccustomed to rowing, managed somehow to tangle herself up in her hair; and in an attempt to free herself lost an ornament of new turquoise, which fell into the water and sank. She ceased to row and the others, following her example, ceased to row as well.

Despite the distractions, Seneferu noticed that the craft had stopped and inquired as to the reason. When the girl told him of the loss of her ornament, he promised that it would be restored to her forthwith and called for the sage Tchatcha-em-ankh who, you will recall, was the originator of the divertissement.

Now Tchatcha-em-ankh was . . . a priest and a writer, both of which might indicate he was a sorcerer as well; and such seems to have been the case. For on hearing the problem, he spoke certain hekau (which is to say, Words of Power) and a great miracle occurred.

On the command of Tchatcha-em-ankh, one portion of the water of the lake went up upon the other, like stones in a building, leaving the bed of the lake dry.

The virgins were fearful of this wall of water, which towered four and twenty cubits, and even Pharaoh glanced about nervously. But Tchatcha-em-ankh walked beneath it dry shod and found the ornament lying upon a potsherd. When he had returned it to the maiden, he then caused the water-wall to break, the water to fall, and the lake to return to its former condition.

The similarity between this ancient tale of magic and the biblical miracle is obvious.

L

AFTER THE EXODUS, Moses again met with his father-in-law, who performed sacrifices and advised him regarding an improved judicial system.

These traditions suggest that certain aspects of Moses' religious and legislative reforms, perhaps even God's new name, Yahweh, were derived from beliefs of the Midianites. The Old Testament claims, however,

that Moses led his people to a sacred mountain, named
Sinai in one source, Horeb in another. There, God ap-
peared in a frightening display of thunder and lightning.
Moses went up into the mountain and returned with
God's instructions in the form of the Ten Command-
ments.

Here too, the Egyptian background of Moses is
clearly underlined. Contrary to popular belief, the Commandments were not unique to emergent Judaism, but
echoed far earlier passages in the Egyptian *Book of the
Dead* where they are the righteous confession of a soul
to the god Thoth. Although male, Thoth was a lunar
deity which suggests connection with the earlier Goddess-oriented culture. He was also the god of magic,
science, craft work, and technology—the four were un-
differentiated in the Egyptian mind. As Graham Hancock
has pointed out in a footnote to his *The Sign and the
Seal*, the parallels between Thoth of the Egyptians and
Yahweh of the Hebrews are too extensive to ignore.

When Moses encountered his "Lord" at the burning
bush, his initiate training would have prompted him to
demand the god's name. Surviving religio-magical texts
make it clear this was standard practice when commu-
nicating with spirits. But the entity in the burning bush
declined to reply. The term JHVH, usually translated as
Yaweh or Jehovah, is not a name, but a refusal to give a
name. It means "I am who I am"—a brusque rejoinder
that only just stops short of telling Moses to mind his
own business.

5

IT IS NOT necessary to accept a religious
viewpoint in order to understand it. It is irrelevant
whether Moses talked with God, a spirit, or an hallucinatory projection of his own unconscious mind. It is
enough that he *believed* himself in contact with a super-

natural entity, for it was the belief that conditioned his subsequent actions.

This is a point that should be put in context. Moses at the burning bush was not the monotheist he later became. He was a man trained in Egypt, which meant belief not in one god, but a whole pantheon. When the Lord refused to give his name, it is feasible that Moses assumed he was in contact with one of the familiar Egyptian gods, such as Osiris, Horus, or Set. He would probably have put the final decision about the god's identity on hold until he had enough information to make up his mind. Meanwhile, he was driven to obey instructions, since his assumption would be they came from some higher authority, even if he was not certain which.

During the forty days and nights Moses remained on the mountain, his Lord not only wrote the Commandments on tablets of stone, but gave extensive instructions on the sort of offerings the Israelites were to make to him:

> And this is the offering which ye shall take of them; gold, and silver, and brass,
> And blue, and purple, and scarlet, and fine linen, and goats' hair,
> And rams' skins dyed red, and badgers' skins, and shittim wood,
> Oil for the light, spices for anointing oil, and for sweet incense,
> Onyx stones, and stones to be set in the ephod, and in the breastplate.
> And let them make me a sanctuary; that I may dwell among them.[4]

There were extraordinarily detailed instructions for the construction of this sanctuary. Ten blue, purple,

---

[4] Exod. 25:3–8.

and scarlet linen curtains each edged with exactly fifty loops were to be joined together with gold thread to form a sort of inner chamber. This was covered by eleven further curtains of goats' hair, joined with brass taches. These curtains were in turn covered with red-dyed rams' skins and undyed badger skins.

Just as detailed instructions were given for another artifact, the Ark of the Covenant:

And they shall make an ark of shittim wood: two cubits and a half shall be the length thereof, and a cubit and a half the breadth thereof, and a cubit and a half the height thereof.

And thou shalt overlay it with pure gold, within and without shalt thou overlay it, and shalt make upon it a crown of gold round about.

And thou shalt cast four rings of gold for it, and put them in the four corners thereof; and two rings shall be in the one side of it, and two rings in the other side of it.

And thou shalt make staves of shittim wood, and overlay them with gold.

And thou shalt put the staves into the rings by the sides of the ark, that the ark may be borne with them.

The staves shall be in the rings of the ark: they shall not be taken from it.

And thou shalt put into the ark the testimony which I shall give thee.

And thou shalt make a mercy seat of pure gold: two cubits and a half shall be the length thereof, and a cubit and a half the breadth thereof.

And thou shalt make two cherubims of gold, of beaten work shalt thou make them, in the two ends of the mercy seat.

And make one cherub on the one end, and the other cherub on the other end: even of the mercy seat shall ye make the cherubim on the two ends thereof.

And the cherubims shall stretch forth their wings on high, covering the mercy seat with their wings, and their faces shall look one to another; toward the mercy seat shall the faces of the cherubims be.

And thou shalt put the mercy seat above upon the ark; and in the ark thou shalt put the testimony that I shall give thee.

And there I will meet with thee, and I will commune with thee from above the mercy seat, from between the two cherubim which are upon the ark of the testimony, of all things which I will give thee in commandment unto the children of Israel.[5]

Whatever Moses subsequently claimed and the Israelites may have thought, this construction was not exclusive to the Hebrews.

6

A SERIES OF faded reliefs on the walls of a colonnade in the great temple at Luxor tell the story of an important religious occasion in the life of Ancient Egypt—the Festival of Apet. In the days of the boy pharaoh Tutankhamen, who ordered the reliefs inscribed, this festival marked the high point of the Nile flooding on which the agricultural life of the country depended. The reliefs show a massive procession in which the populace appear to be involved in an ecstatic act of group worship centered on a number of containers carried shoulder high by priests.

Author and journalist Graham Hancock has remarked on the similarity between the Egyptian ceremony and a procession he witnessed in Ethiopia.

---

[5] *Ibid.* 10–22.

Although a Christian ceremony, the procession obviously drew on the ancient Ethiopian Jewish tradition. To Hancock it was obvious that:

> Both events [the Ethiopian ceremony and the Apet Festival] . . . focused around a kind of "Ark worship," with the Arks being borne aloft by groups of priests and adored by hysterical crowds.[6]

The similarity between these Egyptian "arks" and the Old Testament Ark of the Covenant is not coincidental. When Howard Carter opened Tutankhamen's tomb in 1922, he discovered among other artifacts a number of caskets, fitting one inside the other like Russian dolls. Professor of Egyptology, Kenneth Kitchen, admits the possibility that they—and others like them—may have been design prototypes of the Ark of the Covenant.

Everything in this account suggests the Ark of the Covenant was an elaborate religious artifact—a suggestion readily accepted by generations of theologians and scholars. An entry on the Ark in the *Grolier Electronic Encyclopedia* states that "in ancient Israel's history and cult, it served as a symbol of God's presence. . . ." But there are indications in the Old Testament that it was nothing of the sort.

---

[6] In *The Sign and the Seal* by Graham Hancock, Mandarin Books, London, 1993.

19 | A DANGEROUS ARTIFACT

THE EMERGENT NATION of Israel remained in the desert under Moses' leadership for a number of years, camping at Qadesh and other oases. During that time and later, incident after incident points to the fact that the Ark of the Covenant was not a cult object symbolizing the presence of God, but a weapon of substantial destructive potential. It was a weapon that was dangerous to handle.

Just as the Egyptian practice of using god-names for constellations served to disguise their developed astronomy, so the religious terminology of the ancient Hebrew scriptures serves to disguise the reality of what is being described. The picture is further complicated by the near certainty that the religious terminology ultimately springs from misunderstandings by the Hebrews themselves—misunderstandings that may have been consciously fostered by Moses.

To place the story in context, we have a captive people suddenly freed, but led into the rigorous, threatening conditions of a desert environment. So desperate were they for psychological solace, that they melted down their earrings to make a golden calf that they worshiped as representative of the deities who had helped their escape. At this stage, the rigid monotheism that was to make the Hebrew nation unique in the ancient world was not only unheard of, but literally unthinkable.

The initiate Moses, finding himself at the head of a primitive, undisciplined, and superstitious rabble, may have decided to bring them cultural cohesion through the introduction of a more sophisticated religious impulse. To this end, he created a weapon of war, possibly electrical in nature, that he encouraged the Hebrews to believe contained the life force of a powerful deity. The deity was broadly patterned on the Egyptian Thoth (whom Moses would in any case have associated with a device of this nature) but disguised under the name Yahweh. Even the Egyptian name for this deity, Djhowtey,[1] has faint linguistic similarities to the Hebrew.

2

ALL THIS IS speculation at odds with the conventional picture of emergent Judaism. But there is evidence to support it—especially when it comes to establishing the real nature of the Ark of the Covenant. Louis Ginzberg's monumental study *Legends of the Jews*[2] contains much oral tradition relating to the Ark. This tradition speaks of "sparks" or "fiery jets" that jumped spontaneously from the cherubim and occasionally burned, or even destroyed, nearby objects.

Jewish legend also suggests the intermittent appearance of a field phenomenon (referred to as a "cloud") between the cherubim. When it happened, the Ark was considered so dangerous that even Moses would not approach it. The Israelites thought that at such times their most holy artifact was in the hands of demons. When Moses heard—or claimed to have heard—the voice of God issuing from the Ark, eyewitnesses noted a "tube of fire" was invariably present, sometimes reaching high into the air.

These indications of electrical activity associated with the Ark are supported by a persistent tradition

---

[1] The more familiar "Thoth" is the Greek version of the name.
[2] Jewish Publication Society of America, Philadelphia, 1911.

that the sparks emitted by the artifact occasionally killed people carrying it. Perhaps even more telling, the Ark produced an energy that was capable of flinging people off the ground and sometimes even lifting the Ark itself.

Anyone with experience of a high voltage cable will find these legends hauntingly familiar. If you touch such a cable without insulation you will typically be flung through the air in a shower of sparks. In some cases the shock will be enough to cause death.

∃

THE PICTURE DRAWN in Jewish legend is supported by the biblical account which, to anyone other than the most committed fundamentalist, describes something very different to a typical religious artifact. In Leviticus, for example, there is a detailed—and gory—description of how Moses gathered his followers at the door of the tabernacle to make animal sacrifices:

> And there came a fire out from before the Lord, and consumed upon the altar the burnt offering and the fat: which when all the people saw, they shouted, and fell on their faces.[3]

This "fire," it is clear, emerged from the Ark of the Covenant since that was where the Israelites believed the Lord to dwell. It seems to have been preceded by a glow, which the Bible describes as the "glory of the Lord." It also seems to have been difficult to control, as witness what happened to Moses' own nephews, Nadab and Abihu:

---

[3] Lev. 9:24.

And Nadab and Abihu, the sons of Aaron, took either of them his censer, and put fire therein, and put incense thereon, and offered strange fire before the Lord, which he commanded them not.

And there went out fire from the Lord, and devoured them, and they died before the Lord.[4]

This is a particularly interesting passage since it differentiates between two types of fire—the "fire" generated by the Lord and the "strange fire" made by the two members of the priestly family. But it seems that the fire made by Nadab and Abihu was the familiar kind used for burning incense, so it was the Lord's "fire" we would find different. Why did it reach out to devour the two men? The incident makes no sense at all in religious terms, but makes perfect sense in scientific terms if we assume the censer they carried was made from a conductive metal, such as copper, that would attract an electrical charge.

If all this seems far-fetched, it may be useful to follow the biblical history of the Ark and examine what happened without preconceptions.

L

AFTER CAMPING AT the foot of Mount Sinai for a time, the Israelites eventually left for a new site led by the Ark borne on the shoulders of the priestly Levites. It was a dangerous job, according to Jewish legend, for the Ark contained so much power it was sometimes jerked into the air, carrying its bearers with it. On other occasions it would fling the priests violently to the ground and sometimes even emit sparks that killed them.

During a break in the journey the artifact caused the

---

[4] Lev. 10:1–2.

death of more than a few bearer-priests. According to Numbers:

> And when the people complained . . . the fire of the Lord burnt among them, and consumed them that were in the uttermost parts of the camp.
>
> And the people cried unto Moses; and when Moses prayed unto the Lord, the fire was quenched.
>
> And he called the name of the place Taberah: because the fire of the Lord burnt among them.[5]

It appears only the initiate Moses was capable of switching off this monstrous machine.

5

WHY KEEP SUCH a dangerous item? The answer is that for all its perils, it was useful. Throughout their forty years wandering in the Sinai wilderness, the Israelites discovered that if they carried the Ark into battle, victory was assured. The devout see this as indication that the Creator of the Universe was happy to side with an obscure Semitic tribe in their desert squabbles. At a more sophisticated level, it might seem that faith in their God gave the Israelites sufficient of a moral boost to win their battles. But Jewish legend describes something far more specific:

> An account of one such battle describes the Ark as first uttering "a moaning sound" then rising up off the ground and rushing toward the enemy—who not surprisingly were plunged into disarray and slaughtered on the spot.[6]

---

[5] Num. 11:1–3.
[6] Quoted from *The Sign and the Seal* by Graham Hancock, Mandarin Books, London, 1993.

The biblical account confirms that something of this sort was the norm when Israel went into battle. Certainly the implication is clear that the Israelites carried the Ark into battle as a matter of course:

> And it came to pass, when the ark set forward, that Moses said, Rise up, Lord, and let thine enemies be scattered; and let them that hate thee flee before thee.
>
> And when it rested, he said, Return, O Lord, unto the many thousands of Israel.[7]

The result was that in their barren part of the world, the Israelites grew increasingly powerful at the expense of their neighboring tribes.[8] Nor were they particularly benevolent conquerors. After subduing the Midianites, Moses ordered his officers to murder every male child and mature woman, but to "keep for themselves" the virgin girls.

When Moses died within sight of the Promised Land, leadership of the Israelites and, it would appear, the secret of the Ark, was passed on to Joshua. The artifact was still highly charged and capable of producing some startling effects as shown in the following passage from Joshua:

> And it came to pass, when the people removed from their tents, to pass over Jordan, and the priests bearing the ark of the covenant before the people;
>
> And as they that bare the ark were come unto Jordan, and the feet of the priests that bare the ark

---

[7] Num. 10:35–36.

[8] Truly the Lord hath delivered into our hands all the land; for even all the inhabitants of the country do faint because of us. Josh. 2:24.

were dipped in the brim of the water (for Jordan overfloweth all his banks all the time of harvest),

That the waters which came down from above stood and rose up upon an heap very far from the city Adam, that is beside Zaretan: and those that came down toward the sea of the plain, even the salt sea, failed, and were cut off: and the people passed over right against Jericho.

And the priests that bare the ark of the covenant of the Lord stood firm on dry ground in the midst of Jordan, and all the Israelites passed over on dry ground, until all the people were passed clean over Jordan.[9]

This "miracle," reminiscent of Moses' parting of the Red Sea, is suggestive of a field technology capable of holding back substantial bodies of water. If the field was generated by the Ark, as would seem the case in the foregoing account, then we are examining an even more sophisticated piece of machinery than previously suspected. It was a piece of machinery that Joshua treated with considerable caution. Just before this miraculous crossing of the Jordan (on the way to his famous battle of Jericho) he and the Israelites camped on the banks of the river:

And it came to pass after three days, that the officers went through the host;

And they commanded the people, saying, When ye see the ark of the covenant of the Lord your God, and the priests the Levites bearing it, then ye shall remove from your place, and go after it.

Yet there shall be a space between you and it, about two thousand cubits by measure: come not near unto it, that ye may know the way by which ye

---

[9] Josh. 3:14–17.

must go: for ye have not passed this way hereto-
fore.[10]

Two thousand cubits is a substantial distance—some
1,388 yards, or close on a mile—but Joshua was convinced this was the safety margin required when the
Ark was generating sufficient force to hold back the waters.

Having succeeded in his bid to take Jericho, Joshua
established something of a reign of terror throughout
the neighboring countryside. In this he was consistently
aided "by the Lord":

And the Lord discomfited them before Israel, and
slew them with a great slaughter at Gibeon, and
chased them along the way that goeth up to
Bethhoron, and smote them to Azekah, and unto
Makkedah.[11]

And again, following the destruction of the city of Ai,
which resulted in the slaughter of 12,000 of its citizens
and the hanging of its king:

Then Joshua built an altar unto the Lord God of
Israel in Mount Ebal.

As Moses the servant of the Lord commanded
the children of Israel, as it is written in the book of
the law of Moses, an altar of whole stones, over
which no man hath lift up any iron: and they offered
thereon burnt offerings unto the Lord, and sacri-
ficed peace offerings.

And he wrote there upon the stones a copy of
the law of Moses, which he wrote in the presence of
the children of Israel.

And all Israel, and their elders, and officers, and

----

[10] Josh. 3:2–4.
[11] Josh. 10:10.

their judges, stood on this side the ark and on that side before the priests the Levites, which bare the ark of the covenant of the Lord . . .[12]

This passage not only links the Ark with Joshua's victory, but prohibits bringing metal too close to the artifact—a lesson presumably learned years previously with the deaths of Nadab and Abihu. It is also interesting to note that when Joshua began his campaign against Ai, he neglected to use his most powerful weapon, the Ark of the Covenant, with disastrous results:

And the men of Ai smote of them about thirty and six men: for they chased them from before the gate even unto Shebarim, and smote them in the going down: wherefore the hearts of the people melted, and became as water.[13]

Within a century and a half of Joshua's death, however, the Ark was no longer carried routinely into battle, but remained in a special sanctuary. It is possible that the secret of controlling the Ark's enormous power—not easy at the best of times—may at this late date have been lost.

When the Philistines defeated the Israelites—who had not been carrying their ultimate weapon—at the Battle of Ebenezer, tribal Elders ordered that the Ark be used during the next encounter. This caused consternation among the Philistines but they decided a fight to the death was better than becoming slaves to the Hebrews. Battle was joined, some 30,000 Israelite foot soldiers were slaughtered. Then the Philistines managed to capture the Ark.

---

[12] Josh. 8:30–33.
[13] Josh. 7:5.

6

SUCH AN OUTCOME would have been unthinkable at the time of Moses, or even Joshua. It also creates difficulties for the fundamentalists who argue that the Ark really *was* the seat of God in those distant days—for how could an omnipotent deity permit Himself to be captured so ignominiously?

But religious artifact or electrical machine, there was still energy remaining in the Ark. The Philistines carried their trophy to Ashdod and placed it in their own temple beside a statue of Dagon. The next morning they discovered the statue had fallen facedown on the ground. They replaced it upright, but the following day it had fallen again and this time smashed, with head and hands severed from the trunk.

The Philistines decided they would be safer if the Ark was taken to Gath, but shortly after the artifact reached the town, its citizens suffered an outbreak of tumors. This sounds like the result of radiation, and serious radiation at that. But whether an act of technology or an act of God, it caused such panic that the Ark had to be taken from Gath. The Philistine authorities ordered it sent to Ekron. A further outbreak of tumors promptly occurred in this town, causing such civil unrest that the chiefs of the Philistines were told in no uncertain manner that the Ark must go.

A belated decision was made to return it to the Israelites. It was loaded onto an oxcart along with quantities of gold and jewels as a peace offering and sent to the nearest Israeli-occupied territory, a place called Bethshemesh.

The Philistine chiefs followed at a safe distance up to the border, then allowed the cart to continue unaccompanied. As luck would have it, the cart eventually came to rest in a farmer's field near a megalith. The farmer, ironically called Joshua, recognized the Ark and gathered together a large crowd to make sacrifice on the nearby stone. Levite priests took the Ark and the coffer of treasure from the cart which was then broken up for firewood to be used in preparing a burnt sacrifice of the cattle that had drawn it. Unfortunately the most elementary of all safety precautions was forgotten and the Ark itself was opened. A great many people had crowded around to look inside and seventy of them were struck dead.[14]

The First Book of Samuel 6:20 records the reaction of the Bethshemites to this latest disaster. The King James translation renders the text:

> And the men of Bethshemesh said, Who is able to stand before this holy Lord God? and to whom shall he go up from us?

But the New English version is far less obscure:

> No one is safe in the presence of the Lord, this holy God. To whom can we send it to be rid of him?

In a religious context this is an astonishing passage, but understandable if you view the Ark as a hideously dangerous machine generating electrical field forces that the Israelites believed to be divine power. The Ark was in fact taken to Kiriathjearim and stored in the hilltop house of Abinadab with his son Eleazar appointed as its guardian. There it remained for more than twenty years.

---

[14] The King James version of the Bible puts the number at 50,070, but modern scholars are fairly certain this figure resulted from a mistranslation of the original text.

7

WHEN DAVID BECAME King of Israel, he decided to bring the Ark to Jerusalem to celebrate his most recent victories over the Philistines. But it soon became evident that the intervening years had made the Ark no less dangerous:

And they set the ark of God upon a new cart, and brought it out of the house of Abinadab that was in Gibeah: and Uzzah and Ahio, the sons of Abinadab, drave the new cart.

And they brought it out of the house of Abinadab which was at Gibeah, accompanying the ark of God: and Ahio went before the ark.

And David and all the house of Israel played before the Lord on all manner of instruments made of fir wood, even on harps, and on psalteries, and on timbrels, and on cornets, and on cymbals.

And when they came to Nachon's threshing floor, Uzzah put forth his hand to the ark of God, and took hold of it; for the oxen shook it.

And the anger of the Lord was kindled against Uzzah; and God smote him there for his error; and there he died by the ark of God.

And David was displeased, because the Lord had made a breach upon Uzzah: and he called the name of the place Perezuzzah to this day.

And David was afraid of the Lord that day, and said, How shall the ark of the Lord come to me?

So David would not remove the ark of the Lord unto him into the city of David: but David carried it aside into the house of Obededom the Gittite.[15]

Since it seems inconceivable that God—even so bloodthirsty a God as portrayed by the Old Testa-

---

[15] 2 Sam. 6:3–10.

ment—should execute a man whose only transgression was attempting to steady a holy relic, we are again forced back to the theory that the Ark was not a holy relic at all, but rather a highly dangerous artifact, becoming less and less understood with every passing decade.

Certainly, King David was very wary of it. He left it with Obededom for a full three months before laying claim to it again when no disasters struck the Gittite and his family. Then, taking due note of the safety precautions laid down by Moses, he had the artifact carried in triumph into Jerusalem where it was placed in a tented tabernacle similar to that which had traditionally housed it in the desert.

David's son, Solomon, set about building a new home for the Ark. Although described as a "temple," it had all the hallmarks of a fortress . . . or a protective vault. Moriah, the Mount of Vision, on the east side of the city was the selected site. Its top was leveled and its precipitous sides were faced with a wall of immense stones strongly mortised and wedged into the rock. Around the whole quadrangular area a solid wall of considerable height and strength was built. A second wall encompassed another quadrangle. On the inside of this wall ran a portico over which were built a variety of chambers. Another lower wall separated two inner courts, each at different levels.

It is interesting to note that the ground-plan of the building was based on an Egyptian model, right down to the specific measurements which accord with some of the most ancient temples in Upper Egypt. Why, one wonders, should Israel turn to the architecture of its traditional enemy, the nation that had enslaved its people for so long? It is tempting to speculate that Solomon, renowned for his wisdom, may have suspected the real origins of his most holy artifact and concluded the Egyptians were the only ones with the knowledge to control it.

Certainly no effort or expense was spared to create a safe storage for the Ark. The walls were of hewn stone overlaid, like the floor and ceiling, with gold. The finest and purest was reserved for the sanctuary that would house the Ark. All the vessels to be used, the ten candlesticks, 500 basins, and all the rest of the sacrificial utensils, were also of solid gold. There was also a seventeen-foot diameter tank of molten brass, supported on twelve brass oxen, the purpose of which remains difficult to determine.

The whole structure took more than a decade to build. At the opening, Solomon took his place on a raised throne of brass. Huge crowds of his subjects packed the spacious courts beyond. The ceremony began with the preparation of burnt offerings, in the ancient tradition of the Israelite religion. Then came the installation of the Ark of the Covenant which arrived in procession, borne by the Levites. When the procession reached the Holy of Holies, a chamber built to be completely dark, the veil was drawn back and the Ark set in place on a massive stone slab known as the *Shetiyyah*, or Foundation. At this point, it is recorded that the house was filled with "a cloud" that prevented the priests from carrying out their duties. As had happened so often before, "fire" erupted from the Ark. On this occasion the massive energy charge claimed no lives, but only consumed the animal sacrifices. The celebrations lasted for two weeks, during which 22,000 oxen and 120,000 sheep were slaughtered. When it was over, the doors were closed and the Ark was hidden from all but priestly sight until the time, somewhere between the tenth and sixth centuries BC, when it disappeared from the historical record.

Receipt No. 305042

Shamrock Airport Express

Cheyenne	$32.00
FTC/LVD	$24.00
Longmont	$21.00
Children	$8.00
Door to Door	
Other	

Date 9-10-0

Driver

NOT RESPONSIBLE FOR LUGGAGE

20 | CHINESE CONUNDRUM

THE SCIENTIFIC CONSENSUS insists our current technology evolved in a slow, linear progression from the eoliths of the Old Stone Age to the personal computers of the twentieth century. It must be obvious by now that there is something wrong with this picture.

Nowhere do the cracks show more clearly than in China. An orthodox consensus traces the development of Chinese civilization no further back than about 1600 BC with the establishment of the Shang dynasty, itself seen as the result of linear evolution from a primitive and often savage predynastic era. A brief sketch of this era follows.

The earliest hominid fossils (known as Yuanmou man) were discovered in southwest China and have been dated at 1.7 million years. They were classified as proto-human, but related to modern man. The toolmaker Peking man lived about 500,000 years ago in north China, and by about 25,000 BC, an anatomically modern human, Upper Cave man, was making shell and bone artifacts in the vicinity of Beijing.

The fertile region watered by the Yellow River is generally held to be the cradle of Chinese civilization. Here the switch from a hunter-gatherer economy to an agricultural lifestyle first occurred sometime prior to 5000 BC. The orthodox picture suggests that during the first phase of the Neolithic period (c. 5000–2500 BC), farmers employed primitive cultivation techniques, shifted their villages as the soils became exhausted, and lived in semisubterranean houses. In the second phase (*c.* 2500–1000 BC) agriculture became more advanced and farmers lived in permanent settlements. It was during this period that the Shang Dynasty arose to control a loose federation of settlement groups in the Hunan region of north China from *c.* 1600 BC to *c.* 1027 BC. It is believed that many of the characteristic elements of the Shang, such as bronze-making and writing, were derived from the Near East and other places. There are no signs in this orthodox consensus of any advanced prehistoric civilization.

2

YUANMOU MAN WAS not the shambling ape-man you might imagine from the orthodox reports. He was a tool-user. Scrapers, a stone core, a flake, and a quartz point were found with his remains. He walked erect and there is the possibility he may have used fire.

The official classification of Yuanmou man as *Homo erectus* presents an interesting problem for orthodox science. *Homo erectus* evolved from *Homo habilis*, who in turn evolved from *Australopithecus*. But neither *Homo habilis* nor *Australophithecus* is supposed to have existed outside Africa at the time in question.

The problem is compounded by the discovery, in Xihoudu, of paleoliths and cut and charred bones dated some 100,000 years earlier than the Yuanmou finds. On this evidence alone, it would appear humanity has a longer history in China than the scientific consensus supposes. This is not, perhaps, surprising. The Yale University anthropologist Chang Kwang-chih is on record as saying that "the faunal lists for Ma-pa, Ch'ang-yang, and Liu-chiang finds offer no positive evidence for any precise dating."[1] Another expert, Jean S. Aigner, states:

---

[1] These are hominid remains.

"In south China the faunas are apparently stable, making subdivision of the Middle Pleistocene difficult."

3

UNTIL RECENTLY, archaeologists believed that the earliest Neolithic farming villages (the Yang Shao culture) appeared in the Yellow River valley about 4500 BC. Now a series of newly discovered sites has pushed them back to 6500 BC. Furthermore, the evidence indicates that China's Neolithic culture, which cultivated millet and domesticated the pig, came about without outside influence.

In tandem with this comes the discovery that the people of the late Neolithic, the Lung Shan, lived in walled towns and produced wheel-thrown pottery. Although there is not yet enough archaeological evidence to be definite, these finds suggest a level of civilization. Certainly the Lung Shan culture spread widely in north China and may have been associated with what had long been considered the purely legendary Hsia Dynasty.

The idea that civilization emerged in China only with the establishment of Shang rule produces some of the same difficulties as the idea that dynastic Egypt evolved out of a primitive Neolithic culture in the Nile valley. As in Egypt, the problem is that the Shang culture was simply too advanced. For example, the Shang people had a bronze metallurgy of a technical perfection hardly surpassed in world history. Bronze was used to cast elaborate vessels and weapons, all intricately decorated with both incised and high-relief designs. They also had a distinctive writing system employing nearly 5,000 characters, some of which are still in use today. Shang nobles lived in imposing buildings, went to battle in horse-drawn chariots resembling those of Homer's Greece, and were buried in sumptuous tombs. A sophisticated philosophy based on the complementary forces of *yang* and *yin* was already in place. This philosophy achieved its highest expression in the *I Ching* or *Book of Changes*, which is still revered throughout the Far East today. The *I Ching* contains a system of binary arithmetic developed thousands of years before the birth in 1646 of Gottfried Wilhelm von Leibniz, who is credited in the West with its invention.

This suggests the Shang Dynasty did not after all represent the culmination of an evolutionary process from a primitive Neolithic community. All indicators are that Chinese civilization has a much longer history than the orthodox picture allows.

L,

THE MOST COMMON version of the central Chinese creation myth describes how the Creator, P'an-ku, was born from the Egg of Chaos at a time before heaven and earth came into existence. At the moment of his birth, the egg separated into *yin* (heavy) elements which became the Earth and *yang* (light) elements which rose to constitute the heavens.

Scientific research indicates that the atoms which make up the human body were originally forged by a process of nucleosynthesis in the explosions of stars long before the birth of our solar system. These atoms form the familiar transferric (heavy) elements used in the creation of life. There was, in essence, a separation of light and heavy elements.

For a period of 18,000 years, the distance between heaven and earth increased at the rate of ten feet each day. The Creator, P'an-ku, expanded to fill the gap. When he eventually died, his eyes became the sun and moon, his head transformed itself into the sacred mountains, his body the rivers and seas, and his hair the trees and plants of our planet. The myth describes emergent humanity as the fleas on P'an-ku's body. A rather more agreeable version suggests the deity Nü-kua created mankind out of clay. This reflects Hebrew tradition, in which the name of the first man, Adam, actually means "red clay":

> And the Lord God formed man of the dust of the ground, and breathed into his nostrils the breath of life; and man became a living soul.[2]

But whereas the deity of the Old Testament is wholly and aggressively male, Nü-kua is a goddess. Here, as in the traditions of Ancient Egypt, we have an indication that Chinese myth embodies a folk memory of the universal goddess religion of prehistory.

5

CHINESE LEGENDS ASSOCIATE Nü-kua with her brother Fu-hsi, the primal ruler of China and the first of the Three Sovereigns. Together they brought order to the universe after it had almost been destroyed by the monstrous Kung-kung.

The earliest Chinese are supposed to have been a nomad tribe in the provinces of Shensi, which lies in the northwest of China. They became the first subjects of the Goddess. Having established order, she invented marriage and bonded with her brother who taught his people to hunt, fish, and domesticate animals.

Fu-hsi invented the calendar, musical instruments, and the Eight Trigrams that form the basis of Ancient Chinese philosophy and the *I Ching*. These developments refer to the development of civilization, as does the tradition that Fu-hsi taught his people to breed silkworms, thus establishing the basis of a civilized economy.

Fu-hsi was succeeded by Shen-nung, the second of

---

[2] Gen. 2:7.

the Three Sovereigns, who invented the plough and taught his subjects to grow millet. He established markets throughout the country and investigated the healing value of herbs. He is credited with the invention of writing (of a sort) in that he created a system of knotted strings capable of keeping records.[3] Finally, he was believed to have extended the Eight Trigrams into the 64 Hexagrams that comprise the heart of the *I Ching* as we know it today.

There is one small detail in the traditions of Shennung that suggests he may not have been a wholly mythic figure. He is believed to have died after tasting a poisonous plant while investigating the properties of herbs.

6

THE LAST OF the Three Sovereigns was Huang-ti, the Yellow Emperor. In his story the mythic elements are even less pronounced.

Following Shen-nung's death, a rebellion broke out among the southern tribes, strongly encouraged by his chief minister Ch'ih Yu. Huang-ti stepped in to suppress the revolt and subsequently found the first true Chinese Empire. Huang-ti is credited with the invention of boats, carts, pottery, and armor. He also devised an agricultural calendar. In many ways, he is presented as an early scientist. He is believed to have studied all natural phenomena and is closely associated with the development of chemistry and medicine.

It is possible to put some provisional dating on the legendary developments. The Chinese chronicles place the date of the Creation at 2 million years before the birth of the philosopher Confucius in 551 BC. The chron-

---

[3] A similar system existed in South America prior to the Spanish invasion.

icles divide the past into ten epochs, but prior to the eighth of these there is no authentic history. Fu-hsi is assigned a date of 2862 BC. One of his successors, the Emperor Yao, is dated to 2356 BC and believed to have ruled for 98 years before abdicating in favor of a pious farmer named Shun who ruled for 50 years.

Shun, in his turn, abdicated in favor of an engineer's son named Yü, best noted for his journey to heaven to obtain quantities of magical earth from Huang-ti, the Yellow Emperor. Having returned home, he used the magic earth to build dikes to control the floods that devastated China. He is credited with founding the Hsia Dynasty that ruled for 439 years.

7

UNTIL RECENTLY, the Hsia Dynasty was considered a purely mythic expression of Chinese prehistory, but archaeological finds in the 1970s established its reality. According to *The Cambridge Encyclopedia of China*,[4] its capital was at Erh-li-t'ou in Honan Province. The dating of the Hsia Dynasty is now set tentatively between *c.* 2205 and *c.* 1766 BC. Because written records from the period have not yet been discovered, its origins remain unclear. The period of the Hsia and the succeeding Shang and Chou is known as the three dynasties. During this time the country was composed of numerous coexisting clans, of which the Hsia and the Shang were the most prominent. At the zenith of its power, the Hsia Dynasty ruled over vast areas rich in copper and tin deposits in southern Shansi province—a region of tremendous economic significance in China's Bronze Age.

If Yü and the Hsia Dynasty actually existed, it is possible that some of the even earlier "mythic" figures may

---

[4] Cambridge University Press, 1982.

have existed as well. Chinese scholars certainly believe so. The famous Yellow Emperor is assigned an unlikely, but not actually impossible, rule of 100 years between 2697 and 2597 BC. Other sources shorten this to ninety-eight years.

Interestingly, the Chinese sources trace his ancestry through the female line, a common practice during the ascendancy of the Great Goddess. His mother Fu Pao gave birth to him on the banks of the river Chi, from which he derived his surname. He took his personal name, Yu-hsiung, from his hereditary principality and the village near which he grew up.

But if, like Yü, the Yellow Emperor may have been a real historical personage, how seriously can we take Chinese scholastic claims he was an early scientist?

8

APART FROM EARLY travelers such as Marco Polo, the major Western contacts with China were made in the first half of the nineteenth century. Despite millennia of civilization, an almost overwhelming arrogance and a culture that was exotic to the point of bewilderment, China did not present an impressive face to the West.

By the end of the previous century, symptoms of dynastic decline had begun to appear. Military campaigns on the periphery of the empire required enormous expenditures, and corruption was rampant at all levels of government. The Chinese Empire was geographically far-flung, but it had a seriously weak heart.

With Western contact came conflict, occasioned by disagreements over trade. The Ch'ing Dynasty sought to treat the European powers as vassal states. Diplomatic and commercial relations were seen within the ancient framework of tribute. Foreign trade was strictly confined to the single port of Canton. This did not please the British, the most active of the European traders.

They retaliated with a semiofficial policy of opium smuggling with the twin aims of releasing Chinese goods—opium was the only currency certain to be accepted—and weakening Chinese morale. When the imperial authorities ordered the destruction of all foreign opium at Canton, the British reacted by declaring war— the First Opium War of 1839–42. They had an easy victory. By the time the war ended, the Chinese were forced to cede Hong Kong, open several ports to unrestricted trade, and promise to conduct foreign relations on the basis of equality. They were also compelled to recognize the principle of extraterritoriality, by which Westerners in China were subject only to the jurisdiction of their own country's consular court.

More concessions were wrested from China after the Second Opium War of 1856–60, that saw the foreign occupation and looting of Peking and resulted in the opening of all China to Western representatives. The second humiliation to the Ch'ing coincided with a series of internal rebellions sparked by the decline of central authority.

All this led to a widespread Western perception of China as a feudal kingdom with delusions of grandeur that had known little of real civilization prior to its contact with the West. Such a perception, with some modification, has been retained to the present day. Chinese technology, if we bother to think about it at all, is assumed to have been imported from the West. In fact, nothing could be further from the truth.

٩

In 1942, Dr. Joseph Needham was asked to visit China as an envoy of the Royal Society. He remained for the duration of World War II as Scientific Counsellor at the British Embassy in Chungking. His experience of the country led directly to his embarking on his master work, *Science and Civilisation in China*, the first volume of which was published in 1954. Fourteen further volumes followed and the entire work is projected at twenty-five volumes in total.

Needham's research showed conclusively that, far from being a backward country, the historical debt of Western science and technology to the ingenuity of the Chinese is almost unimaginable.

Robert K. G. Temple, who published the first popularization of Needham's work,[5] estimates that "possibly more than half of the basic inventions and discoveries upon which the modern world rests" arose in China. An examination of these inventions leads to major surprises.

10

THE DECIMAL SYSTEM, a mathematical fundamental of modern science, was in place during the Shang Dynasty dating from 1600 BC. This is not to say the decimal system was invented during the Shang Dynasty. The evidence is that it was inherited from a much earlier date.

The Chinese were using negative numbers, the symbol zero, and decimal fractions long before the birth of Christ. They were able to extract higher roots and find solutions to higher numerical equations that baffled Europeans well into the fifteenth century. The *Nine Chapters on the Mathematical Art*, an early Chinese classic, describes a method of extracting the cube root of 1,860,867.[6] Later works contain equations as complex as $ax^6 + bx^5 + cx^4 + dx^3 + ex^2 + e = 0$.

Essentially the same point needs to be made here as was made about Egyptian astronomy. Sciences do not arise full blown—they evolve. If the Chinese were using

---

[5] *China: Land of Discovery and Invention*, Patrick Stephens Ltd., Wellingborough, England, 1986.

[6] If you're having problems working it out, the answer is 123.

a decimal system prior to the Shang Dynasty—that is to say, during the period of prehistory—it presupposes an even earlier mathematical development.

But early Chinese mathematics is only the beginning of the surprises. There are indications as early as the thirteenth century BC that the Chinese had developed the world's first plastics technology.

11

LACQUER IS A plastic varnish with several remarkable properties. Water and other liquids cannot damage it. It is even immune to strong acids and alkalis. It is heatproof up to about 400°F, insulates against electricity, and is resistant to bacterial attack. There was nothing remotely like it in western technology prior to 1869 when John Wesley Hyatt discovered celluloid.

Excavations in 1976 revealed that Queen Fu Hao had been buried in a lacquered coffin during the thirteenth century BC. Once again, this represents only the earliest date we know of, not the actual date of development.

12

THERE IS EXAMPLE after example of high technology in China at a ludicrously early period. Iron ploughs were in use during the sixth century BC, as was the row cultivation of crops. The circulation of the blood was known in the same period. Advanced brewing techniques, making use of stimulated enzymes, were developed sometime prior to the eleventh century BC. The world's first known magnetic compass was used in the fourth century BC as were poison gas, tear gas, and smoke bombs. "Newton's" First Law of Motion was known to the Chinese at this time. They had even managed manned flight, using kites.

In 1986, Robert Temple wrote:

It is just as much a surprise for the Chinese as for Westerners to realise that *modern* agriculture, *modern* shipping, the *modern* oil industry, *modern* astronomical observatories, *modern* music, decimal mathematics, paper money, umbrellas, fishing reels, wheelbarrows, multistage rockets, guns, underwater mines, poison gas, parachutes, hot-air balloons, manned flight, brandy, whisky, the game of chess, printing and even the essential design for the steam engine, all came from China.[7]

Yet even Temple's list is far from definitive. Cast iron, which did not become widely available in Europe prior to 1380, was being produced in China in the fourth century BC and gave rise to iron pots, hoes, axes, chisels, knives, saws, awls, and figurines. It also gave rise to the "Celestial Axis Commemorating the Virtue of the Great Chou Dynasty with Its Myriad Regions." This monumental structure was built on a base 170 feet in circumference and 20 feet high. From the base a 12-foot-diameter column rose 105 feet into the air. This was topped by a canopy 10 feet high and 30 feet in circumference on top of which stood four 12-foot-high bronze dragons supporting a gilded pearl. Except for the dragons and pearl, the entire structure was of cast iron— 1,325 tons of it. Nor was this the only impressive example of Chinese skill with cast iron. The "Great Lion of Tsang-chou" in Hopei Province remains to this day one of the largest single cast iron objects in the world. It weighs 40 tons and stands 20 feet high.

Chinese astronomy, although different in focus to that of Ancient Egypt, was just as impressive. The Chinese had recognized sunspots for what they were prior

---

[7] Quoted from *China: Land of Discovery and Invention* by Robert K. Temple, Patrick Stephens Ltd., Wellingborough, 1986.

to the fourth century BC. By that time, the first great star catalogs had already been drawn up (without the Egyptian conceit that stars were the physical bodies of gods and goddesses). Chinese records of sunspots represent the oldest and longest continuous series of solar observations anywhere in the world.

13

THE SHEER INGENUITY of Chinese technology is reflected in three inventions still capable of drawing astonished stares today.

The first is the southward-pointing carriage, a two-wheeled vehicle bearing a figurine with one arm extended. The figurine points southward, however the carriage is turned. This is achieved not by use of a magnetic compass (although the Chinese were well aware of magnetism) but by means of a series of differential gears incorporating the principle of cybernetic feedback.

An example of this astonishing navigational aid dates to the third century AD when a large carriage 11 feet long, 11 feet deep, and 9.5 feet wide was constructed. The pointing figure was carved from jade and represented a religious "Immortal." Chinese historians record that the design was originally developed by the Duke of Chou, famed for his commentaries on the *I Ching*. According to an official history:

> The south-pointing carriage was first constructed by the Duke of Chou as a means of conducting homeward certain envoys who had arrived from a great distance beyond the frontiers. The country was a boundless plain in which people lost their bearings as to east and west, so the Duke caused this vehicle to be made in order that the ambassa-

dors should be able to distinguish north and
south.[8]

If this record is correct, it means that the southward-
pointing carriage dates back not to the third century AD,
but to some time in the second millennium BC.

The second of the three inventions may be seen, as a
modern reconstruction, in the Science Museum, London. To outward appearances it is a large bronze urn
with dragon heads set at the cardinal and semicardinal
points. Each dragon holds a bronze ball in its mouth.
The urn rests on a circular plinth on which squat eight
bronze toads staring upward, open-mouthed. While the
device looks like nothing more than an ornate artwork,
it is actually an ancient seismograph. It signaled the occurrence of an earthquake by releasing a bronze ball
from a dragon into the waiting mouth of the toad below.
By checking which ball had fallen, the Chinese could
determine the direction of the earthquake's epicenter.
Again, official histories describe the effect:

> On one occasion one of the dragons let fall a ball
> from its mouth though no perceptible shock could
> be felt. All the scholars at the capital were aston-
> ished at this strange effect occurring without any
> evidence of an earthquake to cause it. But several
> days later, a messenger arrived bringing news of an
> earthquake in Lung-Hsi.[9]

Lung-Hsi, modern Kansu, lay some 400 miles to the
northwest. Although no one is absolutely certain how
the Chinese seismograph worked, modern engineers
can hazard a good guess. But it was not until the 1930s
that Western science solved the puzzle of Ancient
China's "light-penetrating mirrors."

---

[8] *Ibid.*
[9] *Ibid.*

These are handheld mirrors made from bronze. The reflecting side is concave and highly polished. The back, typically, is cast with a picture motif or a series of Chinese ideographs. When the mirror is held up to bright sunlight, it will reflect onto any dark surface the picture on the back, as if the bronze of the mirror had somehow become transparent. There was a trick involved, but such a good one that it had to wait until 1932 for its solution. In that year the British crystallographer, Sir William Bragg, finally figured out how it was done.

By means of a painstaking process involving a mercury amalgam, the Ancient Chinese had duplicated on the reflective surface of their mirrors the same picture that was worked in bronze on the back. But the reproduction was done on such a scale that it could not be detected by the naked eye. Only when enhanced by reflection did the picture appear. Mirrors of this type are known to have existed in the fifth century AD, but yet again, Chinese historians date their development to an archaic period of prehistory.

14

THE BROAD SWEEP of Chinese invention is breathtaking. The following list chronicles just some of the "firsts" developed by this ancient culture.

Belt drives
Biological pest control
Bombs
Cannons
Chain drives
Chain pumps
Chemical warfare
Crank handles
Crossbows
Discovery of the solar
  wind
Double action piston
  bellows
Endocrinology
Fishing reels
Flame throwers
Flares
Geobotanical prospecting
Grenades

Gunpowder
Guns
Helicopter rotors and
  propellers
Hermetically sealed
  research labs
Hexagonal structure of
  snowflakes
Horse harness
Hot-air balloons
Immunization
Kites
Land mines
Land sailing
Magic lanterns
Magnetic remanence and
  induction
Manned flight
Masts and sailing
Matches
Mechanical clocks
"Mercator" map
  projection
Modern seed drills
Mortars
Paddle-wheel boats
Paper

Paper money
Parachutes
Phosphorescent paint
Playing cards
Porcelain
Printing
Relief maps
Repeating guns
Rockets, including the
  multistage rocket
Rotary winnowing fans
Rudders
Sea mines
Sliding calipers
Spinning wheels
Spontaneous combustion
Steel manufacture
Stirrups
Suspension bridges
Umbrellas
Underwater salvage
Use of natural gas
Use of thyroid hormone
Value of *pi*
Watertight ship
  compartments
Wheelbarrows

Although all of these discoveries and inventions predate their appearance in Europe by many centuries, a few are believed by Western authorities to be relatively recent. Land mines, for example, are dated to AD 1277.

But these developments are in a minority. Nothing else on the list is less than 1,000 years old. Most are more than 2,000. Some are more than 3,000. But in each case these are Western scientific datings, based on solid physical or textural evidence of the existence of an invention or practice at a given date. In other words, what we are looking at is the earliest dates *we know of*. In most cases the ancient Chinese texts suggest the actual discoveries were made in archaic times—that is to say, at some stage in Chinese prehistory.

15

THE VAST BODY of Chinese inventions and discoveries requires an explanation. Western experts suggest that the Chinese have some genetic tendency toward creativity, ingenuity, scientific discovery, and engineering skill. But this ignores the fact that since the first contact with the West, such a genetic tendency has been conspicuously absent. Robert Temple makes the point that when the Chinese were shown a mechanical clock by Jesuit missionaries, they were awestruck. They had forgotten it was they who had invented mechanical clocks in the first place.

Since this early contact, China has largely imported its technology. The modernization of China has meant the adoption of Western methods and machinery. This is not, of course, to suggest there have been no new technological developments within China itself, but there is certainly no evidence of the explosive technological creativity that seems to have been characteristic of China's distant past.

But if not a genetic freak, what then? Are we seriously expected to believe that "more than half of the basic inventions and discoveries upon which the modern world rests"[10] arose from a single culture purely by coincidence? Joseph Needham, in his introduction to Temple's book, wrote:

One after another, extraordinary inventions and discoveries clearly appeared in Chinese literature,

---

[10] Robert Temple's estimate.

archaeological evidence or pictorial witness, often, indeed generally, long preceding the parallel or adopted inventions and discoveries of Europe. Whether it was the array of binomial coefficients, or the standard method in interconvention of rotary and longitudinal motion, or the first of all clockwork escapements, or the ploughshare of malleable cast iron or the beginnings of geobotany and soil science, or cutaneous-visceral reflexes, or the finding of smallpox inoculation—wherever one looked there was "first" after "first."[11]

To the Chinese themselves, there is no mystery. For them the roots of their inventions sink deep into archaic times, in the semilegendary activities of the Yellow Emperor or the mythic goddesses who instructed him.

---

[11] *China: Land of Discovery and Invention* by Robert K. Temple, Patrick Stephens Ltd, Wellingborough, 1986.

21 | ANCIENT AIRCRAFT

THE MOST SACRED books of Hinduism are also the oldest body of literature in India. They are called the Vedas, a Sanskrit term meaning "knowledge," and embody a curious mixture of myth, history, and religious thought. Although the written texts date from between 1500 and 500 BC, they reflect a much older oral tradition.

The Vedas consist of four collections of hymns—Rig Veda, Sama Veda, Yajur Veda, and Atharva Veda—addressed to various deities. Other material has accreted around them to form four books of four parts. They contain not only hymns, but also texts on religious ritual, magical formulae, and commentaries called Upanishads, that are concerned with the nature of reality. Alongside the Vedas stand two important semisecular works—the *Mahabharata* and the *Ramayana*, which, with the Vedas, are the principal sources of Hindu social and religious doctrine.

2

THE *MAHABHARATA* IS an epic poem written in Sanskrit, composed of more than 90,000 couplets. Scholars believe it was compiled by various poets and priests between the fifth century BC and the fourth century AD, but an older tradition ascribes it to the legendary sage, Vyasa.

The importance of the *Mahabharata* to a devout Hindu is that its sixth book contains the *Bhagavad Gita* or *"Lord's Song"* which has become one of the most widely studied sacred writings in India. The *Gita* is Krishna's response to questions posed by Arjuna, a warrior prince, concerning his responsibility in good and evil. Krishna, incarnated as Arjuna's charioteer, instructed Arjuna that the world of matter and individual consciousness are grounded in the same reality, that intuition can grasp the ultimate reality, that human beings possess a divine self within a material being, and that the purpose of life is to lead people to unity with the divine.

These ideas are interesting in themselves. The idea that matter and consciousness are grounded in the same reality is identical to the twentieth century discovery of quantum physics that the act of observation can influence the outcome of an experiment. But the fascination they hold for the Indian mind has tended to obscure the fact that the *Mahabharata* is much more than the Lord's Song. In its totality, it purports to relate the turbulent history of a prehistoric kingdom in India called Kurukshetra.

3

THE OTHER GREAT Sanskrit epic of India, the *Ramayana* is generally agreed to be the work of one person—the sage Valmiki, who composed it in the third century BC. It consists of 24,000 rhymed couplets of 16-syllable lines, organized into 7 books and incorporates many ancient legends, including some drawn from the Vedas. Like the *Mahabharata*, it purports to describe events in ancient India, notably the efforts of the royal hero Rama to regain his throne and rescue his wife from the demon King of Lanka.

Both the *Mahabharata* and the *Ramayana* describe a prehistoric culture so technically advanced that it had flying machines and explosive weapons.

L

THE FOLLOWING QUOTATIONS from the *Ramayana* introduces Pushpaka, a marvelous "aerial chariot." Hanuman, the monkey king, is exploring the palace of the Titan leader when:

> The monkey gazed on the vast aerial chariot named Pushpaka which, gleaming like a pearl, planed above the highest building . . . such was the marvelous creation which met the astonished monkey's gaze.[1]

The craft is described as:

> . . . gilden and bright as the sun with its seats of emerald and pearl, its rooms ranged about, silvered all over, its white banners and supports and gilded apartments enriched with golden lotuses which were hung with many bells.[2]

If this passage is to be taken literally, then Pushpaka was something approaching a jumbo jet, or possibly an airship, in size. There are numerous other references to such craft:

> Having prepared that indestructible vehicle, the Chariot Pushpaka, which was as swift as thought, Bibishana stood before Rama and that aerial car that went everywhere at one's will . . . having been placed at his disposal, the magnanimous Rama . . . was astonished.[3]

---

[1] Quoted from *The Ramayana of Valmiki* Vol. II, trans. Hari Prasad Shastri, Shanti Sadan, London, 1992.
[2] *Ibid.*, Vol. III.
[3] *Ibid.*, Vol. III.

There is no doubt at all that it is an aircraft:

> Under Rama's command, that aerial chariot flew
> through the air with a great noise . . .[4]

The epic then details a long flight, a landing, and a second takeoff with Rama describing his aerial viewpoint of various landmarks on the journey from India to Sri Lanka. When they arrive above the city of Lanka, the passengers get out of their seats for a better view.

These are just a few of the many descriptions given in the *Ramayana* of aircraft, flight, and even aerial battles. Some of the craft were capable of holding their own course, like a modern plane on autopilot.

A clear distinction is drawn between travel on the ground and travel in the air: "Cukra proceeded to Militha on foot, although he was able to fly through the skies . . . and over the seas." A similar distinction was made between aerial and horse-drawn land vehicles: "When drawn into battle by those white horses, that chariot looked exceedingly resplendent, like a vehicle celestial that is borne along the sky."

5

DESCRIPTIONS OF AIRCRAFT in the *Ramayana* pale to insignificance against the multitude of weapons described both here and in the *Mahabharata*. Although dealing with the depths of prehistory, the *Mahabharata* nonetheless describes a scene that is far more reminiscent of Europe in the Middle Ages:

> The city was naturally impregnable, with heavy
> walls and watch towers, the moat being bottomless
> and teeming with fish and crocodiles; seven moats

---

[4] *Ibid.*, Vol. III.

there were, impassable, reinforced with spikes . . .
hard to storm because of catapults, war towers,
and rocks . . .[5]

In the same work comes hints of far more advanced
technology. Rama threatens:

I shall attack the ocean with a ruse and press it
back . . . and if he does not show a way, I shall set
it afire with mighty and irresistible missiles that
blaze fiercely with fire and wind.[6]

This is only one example of what the *Mahabharata*
refers to as celestial weapons "used in times of yore," a
particularly suggestive phrase. These weapons included the *agneya* missile described in action as follows:

Pandava angrily loosed the *agneya* missile at the
Gandharva and burned down his chariot. The
mighty Gandharva, deprived of his chariot, tottered
and fell face down, stunned by the brilliance of the
missile and Dhanamjaya seized him by his chap-
leted hairlocks and dragged him, unconscious from
the impact of the missile, toward his brothers.[7]

Elsewhere in the epic is a description of a curious
weapon given to Krsna—a "discus with a thunderbolt in
the center." It seemed to be some form of explosive
missile by means of which he was promised victory not
alone over men but over gods. The *Ramayana* gives a
vivid description of such weapons in use:

---

[5] *Mahabharata* Book 3, translated and edited by J. A. B. van
Buitenen, University of Chicago Press, Chicago, 1975.
[6] *Ibid.*, Book 3.
[7] *Ibid.*, Book 1.

Ravana, his eyes red with fury, loosed his Solar
Weapon whereupon huge and brilliant discs issued
(forth) . . . which, falling, lit up the sky on every
side and the four quarters were consumed by the
fall of those flaming missiles that resembled the
sun, moon, and stars.[8]

There are even hints of something that sounds sus-
piciously like chemical, biological, or atomic warfare:

Pakashana will destroy the territory of that wretch
with a rain of dust for a distance of a hundred
leagues in extent. In the kingdom of Danda, in seven
days all things animate and inanimate will perish
utterly and everything that grows will vanish entirely under the rain of ashes![9]

A passage in the *Mausala Parva* speaks of a weapon
in the shape of an iron bolt that reduced to ashes two
whole tribes. The king of the day was so disturbed by
this weapon that when an example of it was given him,
he had it pounded to fine powder which was then cast
into the sea.

Also described in the Sanskrit texts is Indra's Dart,
sometimes called the Brahma Weapon. This consisted
of a circular reflecting mechanism that first glowed,
then produced a shaft of light of such power that it
consumed its target.

6

In 1903, the Wright brothers made the
world's first powered flight at Kitty Hawk, North Caro-
lina. Just ten years later a curious publication was deposited in the Royal Baroda Library, Delhi. It was an

---

[8] *Ibid.*, Book 3.
[9] *Ibid.*, Book 3.

English language translation by the scholar G. R. Josyer of a Sanskrit document entitled the *Vymaanika-Shaastra*. It purported to describe the construction of aircraft in ancient India and the training of their pilots.

7

ACCORDING TO REPORTS issued by the Press Trust of India in 1952, Mr. Josyer—by then in his eighties and a director of the International Academy of Sanskrit Research in Mysore—had put on display manuscripts several thousands of years old that dealt with high technology subjects such as food processing, high-rise architecture, the creation of synthetic jewels, and the manufacture of aircraft.

Josyer claimed that the original of the manuscript dealing with aircraft had been written down by Maharishi Bharadawaja, a sage in ancient India, who was even then drawing on an oral tradition that had come down from remotest antiquity.

This and other manuscripts came into the possession of the Brahmin Pandit Subbaraya Sastry in the nineteenth century and was eventually shown to Josyer by Venkatrama Sastry, presumably the Pandit's son. Josyer's translation described principles similar to radar, plane to plane radio communication, and spy devices capable of listening in on enemy aircraft.

In 1952, Josyer went even further, showing journalists some drawings commissioned in 1923 on the basis of detailed descriptions in the ancient text. These showed a helicopter cargo plane, enormous passenger planes capable of carrying up to 500 people, and even triple-decked aircraft. ·

8

WESTERN ACADEMICS GENERALLY assume these Indian epics are mythic rather than historical—

examples of early "science fiction." Hindu scholars aren't so sure. They are more deeply aware than their Western counterparts of the literary tradition that distinguishes between mythic and religious allegories on the one hand and works of historical fact on the other. The epics that describe aircraft and advanced weaponry in ancient India have been categorized as historical.

9

IN 1988, Dr. Kunwarlal Jain Vyas told delegates at a Historical Conference in Delhi that Prince Rama of the *Ramayana* epic actually existed and ruled around 5000 BC. Other papers read at the conference seriously proposed that the roots of Indian civilization dated back some 31,000 years, a figure close to Manetho's dating for the Demi Gods/Horus-Kings of prehistoric Egypt.

10

WHETHER MYTHIC OR HISTORICAL, much of the action of the *Ramayana* takes place over the island of Lanka, modern Sri Lanka, which was supposed to have been the home of Rama's archenemy Ravana. The orthodox history of Sri Lanka begins in the sixth century BC with an invasion by the forces of a northeast Indian prince named Vijaya. The newcomers had little difficulty subduing the aboriginal inhabitants, known as Yakkhas and Nagas.

Tribal descendants of both nations still survive in remote areas of the island today. They form a nomadic hunter-gatherer community, living in caves and rough, portable shelters. Hardly surprising, a long-held assumption was that prior to Vijaya Sri Lanka supported nothing better than a Stone Age culture. But the evidence does not bear this out.

British excavations in the late nineteenth century showed the ancient city of Anuradhapura once had an extremely sophisticated irrigation and discharge system. These were dated to the fourth century BC, 200 years after the invasion. According to the Sri Lankan archaeologist A. D. Fernanado, this dating is in error. The actual engineers were the supposedly primitive Yakkhas.

In an article in the *Journal of the Royal Asiatic Society* in 1982, Dr. Fernanado claims Anuradhapura was originally founded by the Yakkhas at a far earlier date than is currently allowed. They had developed an advanced civilization with its capital in the city of Lanka, the location of which is now unknown, and were celebrating the marriage of their king's daughter when the invaders struck.

One of the great Buddhist histories, the *Mahawamsa*, which attributes the building of Anuradhapura to Prince Vijaya, nonetheless allows that the Yakkhas were skilled in metallurgy—an unlikely talent for a tribe of nomadic hunter-gatherers.

It is equally unlikely that primitive tribesmen built the prehistoric fortress of Ariththa, which used massive worked stone blocks 18 feet by 6 feet by 2 feet thick. Nor were they likely to have built the currently unexcavated city of Vijithapura which aerial survey shows to extend over 250 acres.

Further evidence of sophisticated engineering skills in prehistoric Sri Lanka arose when the Gal Oya Dam Project got under way in the 1950s. As work started, earth moving machinery quickly hit on the remnants of an ancient dam at exactly the same spot. The well-known author and traveler Thor Heyerdahl was among a group of Scandinavian archaeologists who investigated the structure. He later reported that it "would have impressed a pharaoh." When operable, the prehistoric dam had regulated the distribution of billions of gallons of water through a series of artificial lakes.

There were more than 6 miles of sluices and tunneling 33 feet high constructed from 15-ton stone blocks.

11

ON THE INDIAN mainland, archaeological evidence suggests the Indus civilization, which existed from about 2700 to 1750 BC, was one of the most extensive known. It stretched from north of the Hindu Kush down the entire length of the Indus and beyond into peninsular India. To the west it spread close to the present Iran-Pakistan border.

This civilization was sufficiently advanced to develop writing, engraved on fine stone seals, but the script remains undeciphered, so the only hard evidence we have is archaeological.

At one time the civilization was believed to have been established by diffusion from more advanced cultures in Mesopotamia and the Iranian plateau, but recent excavations at Mehrgarh, on the Bolan Pass, show large settlements as early as 7000 BC. Scholars differ as to whether these early settlements evolved directly into the urban communities of the Indus civilization, but this is certainly the favorite theory. It is clear that by about 3200 BC large villages were being formed along the entire course of the river. The first cities of the Indus were discovered accidentally during railroad construction in the mid-nineteenth century, but excavations only began in the 1920s. They revealed a civilization roughly contemporary with Ancient Egypt.

12

AMONG THE MOST important sites were the twin cities of Mohenjo-Daro and Harappa, excavated by Sir Mortimer Wheeler after he became director general of Archaeology in India in 1944. Mohenjo-Daro is situated about 320 kilometers (200 miles) north of Karachi in what is now Pakistan. Harappa is located 640 kilometers (400 miles) northeast of Mohenjo-Daro, in the Punjab of India.

They were cities that showed an astonishingly high level of technical, architectural, administrative, and engineering skill. This did not manifest in the sort of incredible megalithic engineering seen in Mesoamerica—both cities were built almost entirely of kiln-fired brick—but they were obviously preplanned.

Mohenjo-Daro was laid out to a grid pattern with twelve main traffic arteries each between 30- and 45-feet wide dividing the city into a dozen blocks. One of these blocks consisted of a high citadel to the west set on an artificial mound some 20 feet high. There are three major structures on the mound and while their functions are not absolutely certain, they are now commonly called the Granary, the Assembly Hall, and the Great Bath.

The last of these comprises a sort of 8-foot deep swimming pool measuring 40 feet by 23 feet and sunk into the supporting platform. There are traces of wooden steps leading down to it at each end and wooden rooms (which may have been changing rooms) surrounding it. The pool was rendered watertight with gypsum.

The citadel overlooked the remaining eleven blocks of the city that comprised standardized, closely packed brick houses, shops, and workshops. Overall, these houses were rather better designed than many dwellings in our modern cities. A typical layout set several rooms around a central courtyard with no windows overlooking the main streets. Many of the buildings were two-story, some were three.

The culture that created this metropolis was centered on the worship of the prehistoric Great Goddess—many small figurines have been discovered. Despite clear indication of central planning, archaeologists have yet to discover the slightest evidence of central *control*. There does not seem to have been a ruling class or even a priesthood. As in Ancient Egypt, weapons technology was limited and of poor quality. In other areas, however, standards were unexpectedly high. The Indus people supported themselves by an irrigation-based agriculture. They grew domesticated rice, wheat, and barley, and may have cultivated dates and cotton. They were among the first people in the world to keep chickens. It is certain they had domesticated dogs, buffalo, and cattle. They may possibly have had domesticated pigs, horses, camels, and elephants as well.

Archaeologists have long commented on the uniformity and standardization of the civilization. Except in the most remote colonies, the cities were all built of baked-brick blocks with a standard proportion of length to width to thickness of 4:2:1. Pottery forms and designs were also remarkably similar throughout the whole vast area. Today, these findings would be indicative of mass production.

13

THERE WAS AN astonishing sophistication in urban sanitation. In Mohenjo-Daro, this was provided by an extensive system of covered drains running the length of the main streets and connected to most of the residences. There was obviously municipal maintenance of the sewerage since there were manholes at regular intervals. House drains were enclosed clay piping and some houses even had built-in lavatories, with seats. All this suggests a knowledge of hygiene far in advance of anything seen in Europe before the eighteenth century—and anything widely established in Europe before the nineteenth. Such knowledge would have had a carryover effect on the general health of the population.

14

IF IT SEEMS a long way from indoor lavatories to the atomic weapons mentioned in the Hindu
epics, it may be useful to note that the time period in
our own culture was less than 200 years. The modern
water closet was pioneered in 1775 by the London
watchmaker Alexander Cumming. The first atomic
bomb was successfully tested at Alamogordo, New Mexico, in 1945.

There are indications of individuals in ancient India
who understood nuclear and subnuclear physics as
well, if not better, than today's physicists. The man who
first pointed this out was himself a physicist. Dr. Fritjof
Capra qualified at the University of Vienna before undertaking research posts in high-energy physics at several European and American universities. He had
already come to suspect the existence of parallels between the findings of quantum physics and the teach-
ings of Eastern mysticism when he was plunged into an
experience that provided personal confirmation.

I was sitting by the ocean one late summer after-
noon watching the waves rolling and feeling the
rhythm of my breathing, when I suddenly became
aware of my whole environment as being engaged
in a gigantic cosmic dance. Being a physicist, I
knew that the sand, rocks, water, and air around me
were made of vibrating molecules and atoms and
that these consisted of particles which interacted
with one another by creating and destroying other
particles. I knew also that the earth's atmosphere
was continually bombarded by showers of "cosmic
rays," particles of high energy undergoing multiple
collisions as they penetrated the air. All this was
familiar to me from my research in high-energy
physics, but until that moment I had only experi-

enced it through graphs, diagrams, and mathematical theories. As I sat on that beach, my former experiences came to life; I "saw" the atoms of the elements and those of my body participating in the cosmic dance of energy; I felt its rhythm and I "heard" its sound, and in that moment I *knew* that this was the Dance of Shiva, the Lord of Dancers, worshiped by the Hindus.[10]

Dr. Capra's intuition points only to an ancient understanding of subnuclear structure. Some archaeological discoveries point to a possible practical application.

15

MOHENJO-DARO MEANS "Mound of the Dead" and the city lived up to its grisly name when Mortimer Wheeler's team of archaeologists reached into its deeper levels. There they found literally hundreds of skeletons strewn along the ancient streets. Some had met their death holding hands. The same peculiarity was discovered at the comparable level of Harappa. Clearly, some widespread disaster had overcome these cities at one time. The possibility of plague cannot be ruled out—the dead were left unburied in the streets of many medieval European cities during the Black Death.

But there are indications of an even more ominous, if far more fantastical, fate. "Black stones" in their thousands were discovered at Mohenjo-Daro. On analysis they were found to be fragments of clay pottery fused together by the action of intense heat.

[10] Quoted from *The Tao of Physics* by Fritjof Capra, Fontana Books, London, 1975.

| # MARTIAN SEED

CARL SAGAN, who did not believe the structures on Cydonia Mensae were built by ancient Martians, or any other intelligence for that matter, once remarked that "exceptional claims require exceptional proofs."

There can be few more exceptional claims than that the human race originated on the planet Mars and we, unknown to science and ourselves, are colonial descendants.

If you will forgive a personal insertion at so late a stage, I have to admit to some embarrassment at putting forward the idea. For years astronomers have told me Mars was a dead planet—and until very recently every shred of evidence suggested that it always had been. Had I been alive in 1938 when Orson Welles made his famous *War of the Worlds* broadcast announcing a Martian attack on New Jersey, I should not have joined in the panic. I have always known there are no such things as Martians. I find it difficult to believe there ever were. I find it even more difficult to believe Martians look like you and me. If the idea cropped up in science fiction, I would throw the book aside as too naive for my taste. Should Martians ever invade *Star Trek*, I would expect them at the very least to sport Klingon brow ridges, green skin, and Vulcan ears. But all this is no more than one author's mind-set. The evidence is something else.

There is evidence for ancient life on Mars. It was microscopic life, but that's a lot more than was crawling around on Earth at the time . . . or for many millions of years. Then there is the "Face," and other structures at Cydonia.

In the early chapters of this book I presented the evidence that suggests the complex may be artificial. I have not presented the evidence against for a disappointing reason. I have read a great many critiques of Professor Stanley McDaniel, Richard Hoagland, Dr. Mark Carlotto, and the rest. Not one of them amounts to anything more than the position that these things *can't* be artificial, therefore they *aren't* artificial. This is not an application of the scientific method. It is a statement of belief. The belief is defended by attacks on the methodology (sometimes the intelligence) of those who take a different view.

That curious experiment carried out by the Russians is intensely interesting. It shows a wholly unexpected compatibility between the Martian and terrestrial ecospheres. Terrestrial plants can survive (although not reproduce) in both. Insects and even reptiles can survive far longer than anyone would have expected. It is very difficult to accept this has come about purely by chance.

The Martian "meteorite" that looks like a wall has its own level of interest. Although perhaps the least publicized of all the anomalous finds, it is in many ways the most intriguing. First of all, it is utterly unlike any other meteorite to land on Earth. Meteorites vary in size, but their common denominator is that they are round, like oranges or footballs. The thing that came down in the Antarctic is a rectangular stone block. The experts are quite satisfied it came from Mars, but it *looks* as if it were thrown out of a shattered building at Tiahuanaco. Nobody has yet commented believably on what sort of natural action creates a rock that looks like four stone bricks fused together. All this is worthwhile evidence, but it certainly does not constitute proof, let alone the "exceptional proof" Carl Sagan demanded. That point has been made repeatedly by Professor McDaniel. The evidence is suggestive, but not conclusive. He wants NASA to go back up there and take another look. Which is the problem. The scientists find it even harder than I do to believe in the possibility of Martian engineering. But if the evidence of an ancient Martian civilization is so far limited, the same cannot be said for the evidence of a prehistoric civilization on Earth.

2

IN 1508, Martin Baumgarten, a European traveler, discovered in the mountains of Lebanon the ruins of a Roman temple built on such a grand scale that it surpassed any Roman structure in Italy. This temple and various other buildings in the Lebanon complex were erected some 4,000 feet above sea level. Sir Mortimer Wheeler, the British archaeologist who did such sterling work in India, visited the area and subsequently reported: "The temples . . . stand passively upon the largest known stones in the world."

The Romans began work at the site around 63 BC, shortly after they occupied Lebanon. But prior to their arrival, there was a history of building stretching back into the mists of antiquity. Archaeologists accept that at least six other temples had been raised on the spot. The immediate predecessors of the Romans were the Greeks, who believed the area to be holy and built there too. Both Greeks and Romans used as their foundations an enormous paved platform dating back to an unknown, archaic, local culture. The platform extended for more than five million square feet and was, according to a French archaeological mission in the 1920s, built as part of an infrastructure of monumental vaults, caverns, and tunnels deep beneath. This subterranean maze has not yet been fully investigated, but in the nineteenth century, German archaeologists reported the existence of a 460-foot-long vaulted passage comparable in size and sophistication to a modern railway tunnel.

The platform itself is made up of several courses of worked stone blocks ranging in weight up to 500 tons. This makes them more than twice the weight of the largest blocks found in the Great Pyramid. At one point of the complex, three granite slabs have been fitted together with great precision. Each is more than 60 feet long and weighs around 1,000 tons. The stones were quarried three quarters of a mile from the site. At the quarry itself lies a worked block not fully separated from the bedrock. It is estimated to weigh in excess of 1,200 tons. Blocks of this size could be quarried today, but they could not be moved even using modern heavy mechanical equipment. Someone in prehistoric Lebanon managed to move three of them up a mountain, then lay them to a precision of which a modern mason would be proud. The great stones of Lebanon confirm absolutely what might be suspected from an examination of ancient structures in Egypt and South America. Engineering skills in the distant past were actually greater than those at our command today.

3

IN 1936, archaeologists investigating the 5100-year-old tomb of Prince Sabu at Saqqara in Egypt discovered a puzzling object delicately carved from a particularly brittle type of rock known as schist. The object was a type of wheel with a hole through the center, as if it was meant to be fitted over an axle. Since stone wheels could not have been used in this way, there has been speculation that the archaeologists were looking at a representation of something originally made from metal. In metal, the artifact has the functional appearance of a light-rimmed flywheel developed in 1978 in America for transport applications.

An Olmec fragment found in the early 1960s and

dated earlier than 1000 BC turned out to be part of a geomagnetic compass.

At the turn of the twentieth century, Greek divers off the island of Antikythera brought up from a sunken ship a sophisticated mechanical calculator dating back to the first century BC.

In 1898 archaeologists discovered a wooden model of an airplane dated to about 200 BC in a tomb at Saqqara. It has the same wing form and proportions as the Concorde.

L

THE POET HESIOD, writing at a time of turmoil in his own land, harked back to a gentler age when "the fruitful earth poured forth her fruits unbidden in boundless plenty." This idyll was enjoyed by a "golden race" who "In peaceful ease . . . kept their lands with good abundance, rich in flocks and dear to the immortals."

For Hesiod these pure spirits were replaced by a "race of silver" then by a "race of bronze" sprung from shafts of ash. They ate no grain and had hearts of flint. Their major preoccupation was with Ares, the god of war.

The race of bronze conquered the race of silver and their descendants constituted a fourth race of humanity, distinct from those that had gone before and, according to Hesiod, rather more noble. But then there appeared a wicked fifth race whose character was summed up in the words "Right shall depend on might and piety shall cease to be."

All this sounds like myth-making, but historian John Mansley Robinson is prepared to accept that Hesiod's last three "races" at least were actual historical peoples.

The first of these, the "race of bronze," were northern invaders who rampaged around 2000 BC, deriving their name from the fact they carried bronze weapons. Today they are known as the Achaeans. They settled the mainland, built fortresses, then expanded south toward Crete and east to the coast of Asia Minor where they sacked Troy around 1200 BC.

Hesiod's fourth race was the direct result of a culture clash between the invaders and the people they conquered, the agriculturally based culture of Old Europe. The barbaric ways of the Achaeans were modified by the more civilized customs of the settled farmers and the result was a hybrid breed more gentle than the Achaeans.

The fifth race, whom Hesiod despised so much he wished he had died before it emerged, was the Dorians. They were a people who migrated into Greece sometime after 1200 BC by way of ancient Illyria, Epirus, and northeastern Macedonia. Their use of the iron sword helped bring an end to the civilization of the Mycenaeans, that was otherwise far superior to their own.

If three out of Hesiod's five races can be positively identified in this way, then it is entirely possible his first two races were also poetic descriptions of actual peoples whose origins reach back into the mists of prehistory. Seen in this way, not only Hesiod's writings, but other myths and folk tales take on a new light.

5

ONE COMMON DENOMINATOR of Golden Age myths is the emphasis not simply on abundance, but on *agricultural* abundance. Conventional wisdom has it that hunter-gatherer communities existed from 2.5 million years ago, but from about 11,000 to 8000 BC a change began to occur as flint-edged wooden sickles were used to gather wild grains, which were then stored in caves.

In Mesopotamia, cultivation began in the ninth millennium BC. The wheel was invented, pulleys were used to draw water from artificial canals, and complex irrigation systems were constructed. Mesopotamians raised wheat and other cereal grains. They were skilled in gardening and domesticated the camel, donkey, and horse. From approximately 8300 to 6500 BC, other groups began to practice natural plant husbandry by broadcasting seeds and waiting for the harvest. This led to the practice of cultivating plants which was established in the Near East and Europe about 6500–3500 BC, in Southeast Asia about 6800–4000 BC, and in Mesoamerica and Peru about 2500 BC. Mesopotamian tablets show the people took no credit for their early development of agriculture. They insisted that the techniques of planting and harvesting were *taught* to them.

Linguistic analysis has shown the words for *plough, furrow*, and even *farmer* in Sumerian texts are not Sumerian words. They appear to have been taken over from an earlier culture, that, presumably, specialized in agriculture. There are no native Sumerian words for *potter, mason, smith, weaver, leathermaker*, or *basketmaker* either. Here again, the words used in the texts seem to have been drawn from some earlier culture.

A swath of "myths" indigenous to our earliest known civilizations insist that the arts of architecture and town planning were handed down from ancient times, as were legal systems, religious practices, astronomy, navigation techniques, drama, writing, and commerce.

6

IN 1931, two French anthropologists moved in with a primitive Sudanese tribe called the Dogon. Like many tribal people, the Dogon had a two-tier religious structure—the faith practiced by the common people and a secret body of doctrines taught only to special initiates. Fifteen years after joining the life of the tribe, one of the anthropologists, Marcel Griaule, became an initiate.

The secrets that were then revealed to him proved quite extraordinary, for they had little to do with the sort of tribal creation myths one might confidently expect. Instead, they were almost exclusively concerned with astronomy.

Griaule discovered that Dogon initiate doctrine, dating back countless generations in the history of the tribe, taught the Earth and planets orbited the sun— something unknown in Europe until the publication of Copernicus's *De Revolutionibus Orbium Caelestium (On the Revolutions of the Heavenly Spheres)* in 1543. Dogon initiates were aware of the moons of Jupiter, invisible to the naked eye and only discovered in 1609 by Galileo following the invention of the telescope.

The Dogon also knew about the rings of Saturn, first interpreted by Christian Huygens, in his *Systema Saturnium* published in 1659. They were aware the moon was a dead, dry, airless body and had records of the movements of Venus—another area of observation that in Europe had to await Galileo.

But the real surprise the Dogon had for their French initiate was the ancient story that the star Sirius had a tiny companion which was dark, dense and very, very heavy. The reason for its weight was that it was composed of matter heavier than any found on Earth. It moved in an elliptical orbit that took fifty years to complete. It was not unexpected that the Dogon should have noticed Sirius. It is, after all, the brightest star in the night sky with an apparent magnitude only eight times less than that of the full moon. But the idea of an invisible companion was something else.

It was only in 1834 that the German astronomer Friedrich Bessel noticed the proper motion of Sirius was sinuous, and inferred the existence of an unseen companion. In 1862, Alvan Clark discovered that companion, now called Sirius B, while using the Dearborn Observatory's refracting telescope.

In 1928 (just three years before the anthropologists

visited the Dogon) Sir Arthur Eddington first postulated his astronomical theory of white dwarfs—stars that are nearing the end of their lives, having exhausted the hydrogen and helium in their interiors. They are thought to be the final evolutionary stage for stars whose masses are less than 1.4 times that of our sun. Their future is to cool down very slowly until they become black dwarfs, unable to radiate any more energy.

Several hundred white dwarf stars are now known. They have radii about $1/100$ the solar radius, their absolute visual magnitudes are mostly in the range +10 to +14, their surface temperatures range from 4,000 to 25,000°K, and their mean densities are high—approximately a million times that of water. One of them is Sirius B. It is about the size of Earth and it weighs as much as the sun. It has an elliptical orbit that takes fifty years to complete.

There is absolutely nothing in Dogon culture to explain how the tribal initiates came by this accurate and detailed information. They do not practice astronomy and even if they did, it is difficult to see how they could have worked it all out without powerful telescopes and/ or an advanced knowledge of astrophysics. The Dogon claim the knowledge was given to them by a god who came down to Earth from the heavens.

7

THE MYTH OF god-like visitors to Earth in ancient times is as widespread as the myth of the Golden Age itself. To the Australian Aborigines, whose nomadic culture remained virtually unchanged for 40,000 years, they were the Wandjina or Sky People. Portrayed in rock paintings, the Sky People look like astronauts in space suits.

To the Egyptians, Greeks, Sumerians, Aztecs, and every other ancient civilization, the "sky people" were gods. But they were gods only in terms of their power.

In personality and morals they were all too human. The tales of Olympus, in whatever culture they appear, are full of sex, greed, jealousy, and violence. They read like human history. A Hittite text tells how Alalush the king was served for nine years by his subject Anush who then betrayed him in an unexpected coup. Alalush was defeated and fled. Anush seized the throne. But the throne was the throne of heaven and Alalush fled not to another country, but to another planet:

Alalush was defeated
He fled before Anush
Down he descended to the dark-hued Earth
Anush took his seat upon the throne.

Erich Von Daniken went so far in promoting the idea of gods as ancient astronauts that no archaeologist who values his scientific reputation would dare to contemplate it seriously today. But around the time Von Daniken's first English language translation was published, the respected British archaeologist, Tom C. Lethbridge, was putting the finishing touches to his own manuscript *Children of the Gods*. Working independently, Lethbridge had decided there was more than enough evidence to support the suggestion that creatures from another planet had once visited our own.

Lethbridge, like Von Daniken, ignored two great problems with the theory. The first was where the "gods" came from.

In the 1960s, when Von Daniken's fame was at its height, there seemed no question but that we were alone in the solar system and always had been. This meant the home planet of the visitors had to orbit a distant star. Astronomers, well aware of the distances involved, questioned how, when the speed of light was absolute, such a journey could be made. They also questioned, perhaps more tellingly, why distant aliens would bother. Since 1897 we have been announcing our presence to the universe with radio and later with television broadcasts. At the time when the ancient astronauts were supposed to have visited, the Earth was a silent planet.

The second problem was, if anything, more difficult. The myths on which Von Daniken and Lethbridge drew made it clear that the god-like visitors were not simply humanoid, but human. They were so close to terrestrial humanity that the two races were actually able to interbreed:

> . . . when the sons of God came in unto the daughters of men, and they bare children to them, the same became mighty men which were of old, men of renown.[1]

The chances against the evolutionary processes of another planet producing creatures with the same genetic structure as ourselves are literally astronomical.

Faced with those odds, you have only two choices. One is to abandon the idea of human visitors from beyond the Earth. The other is to investigate the possibility that terrestrial humanity itself might have been the result of seeding.

8

IN 1995, two wholly new types of bacteria were discovered. One turned up in an oil reservoir under Paris, France, the other in a deep aquifer near the Columbia River in Washington State.

The bacteria were part of ecosystems that had no dependence on sunlight or even heat. They were driven by chemical reactions between water and basalt. With an instinct for the memorable, scientists now call this

---

[1] Gen. 6:4.

type of mini-ecology a Subsurface Lithoautotrophic Microbial Ecosystem.

Two scientists from the Pacific Northwest Laboratory in Richmond, Washington, James McKinley and Todd Stevens, who have been researching these newly discovered systems, believe that life of a similar type may have developed long ago on Mars. They point to the fact that SLMEs are better adapted to survive under extreme Martian conditions than life systems using photosynthesis.

Since 1962, when the first positive identification of a Martian meteorite was made in Nigeria, scientists have discovered that approximately 500 tonnes of Martian material falls to Earth each year. There have been times in the past when the figure was probably much higher, like the period of intense meteor bombardment that chipped the fossil-bearing Allen Hills meteorite from the Martian surface.

Potentially, any Martian fragment from the period may have started off carrying living bacteria. The question has always been whether such microscopic life could survive passage through the Earth's atmosphere and impact with the ground. Until the discovery of SLMEs, the most likely answer was no. But SLMEs are pre-adapted to far more extreme conditions than any bacteria scientists considered earlier.

Recent studies of a Canadian crater resulting from a 2-billion-year-old impact have unearthed tiny carbon-based spheres containing gases with the spectrum signature of a red giant star. This shows the spheres were not created by the impact, but actually survived it. Since the impact itself generated temperatures of around 5000°C and carbon molecules disintegrate at 1000°C, we have clear proof that carbon-based life forms (the foundation of all life on Earth) could have arrived safely from space. This being so, some scientists now accept the possibility that life on our planet received a jump-start from Mars. A seeding by more evolved Martians is unlikely, but not entirely impossible.

9

THE VICTORIAN SUPERSTITION of uniformitarianism was mainly supported in its own day by the prestige of one distinguished geologist. Even then it failed miserably to explain several troublesome discoveries.

Charles Darwin, who desperately needed uniformitarianism to underpin his own theory of a gradual biological evolution, admitted the Siberian mammoths were a mystery he simply could not explain. For lack of an explanation, he chose to ignore the mystery and held to his original, unmodified theory. Generations of scientists have followed his example. Whether they can continue to do so for much longer is questionable.

The twin bastions of geological uniformitarianism and evolutionary theory demand slow, gradual change and linear growth. Our present civilization, with its widespread use of electricity, global air transport, computer controls, and limited space flight, is seen as the peak of a technological pyramid that began the day some specimen of *Homo Habilis* picked up a stone to crack a nut. There was a slow, gradual climb out of the primitive darkness into the light of modern science. The New Stone Age was more enlightened, more sophisticated than the Old Stone Age. The civilization of Ancient Rome was more technically advanced than the civilization of Ancient Sumer because it was more recent. Eighteenth century Britain was a further step ahead. Progress has always been gradual and one way. There can be no going back.

Even the fully documented historical lesson of the Dark Ages has done nothing to dent the uniformitarian superstition. There is no controversy about the fact that for centuries after the collapse of the Roman Empire, the march of progress not only stopped, but actually reversed its course. The light of learning went out all over Europe and the world sank into a new barbarism when compared with the culture of classical times.

As the weight of evidence continues to increase, it is only a matter of time before the doctrine of uniformitarianism has to be abandoned. When this happens, the orthodox consensus will at long last be able to contemplate unemotionally where the evidence points. For anyone not locked into doctrine, it must be already clear that Sumer was not the first human civilization. A developed culture was in place on our planet by 10,000 BC and seems to have been established at a far earlier date.

While no definitive proof has been forthcoming, a mass of circumstantial evidence suggests the prehistoric civilization reached levels of science and technology comparable to our own. In at least one area— engineering—the ancient civilization managed to surpass us.

If the "Face on Mars" proves to be artificial, there are only two real possibilities. One is that our prehistoric civilization developed space travel and flew to Mars. The other, supported by worldwide mythic tradition and at least some hard archaeological evidence, has the process moving in the opposite direction. This theory calls for the evolution of an advanced Martian civilization at some point in the distant past. It was this civilization that built the structures at Cydonia and created the "Face" out of the same sort of hubris that persuaded Rameses II to commemorate his features in the great rock temple at Abu Simbel.

If the earliest of our anomalous finds prove genuine, then representatives of the Martian civilization found their way to Earth at a period so remote that indigenous life was primitive indeed. The colony came later.

Mars is a dead planet today. At some stage the ancient civilization, in common with all Martian life, died out. But the colony survived. That colony was our Martian Genesis.

EPILOGUE

IN SEPTEMBER 1992, NASA embarked on a new mission to map the Martian surface. That date marked the launch of *Mars Observer*. The spacecraft carried a host of scientific instruments and was designed to photograph the planet from orbit. On August 21, 1993, only days away from Mars, *Observer* suddenly stopped broadcasting.

Conspiracy theorists posted bulletins on the Internet claiming NASA had purposely disabled the craft to avoid having to rephotograph the Cydonia "Face." Others suggested *Observer* had been shot down by aliens.

NASA set up a review board which spent several months investigating the loss. They eventually concluded there must have been a critical failure in the propulsion system. They believe *Observer* flew right past Mars and is now somewhere in orbit around the sun.

2

TOWARD THE END of 1996, NASA tried again. As part of an aptly named Discovery program, the spacecraft *Global Surveyor* was launched toward Mars in November. A month later, a second craft, *Mars Pathfinder*, left the launch pad.

On Friday, July 4, 1997, *Mars Pathfinder* touched down at 19° 33′ North, 33° 55′ West in the Ares Vallis region of the Martian surface.

It was an undignified landing. To protect the costly instruments inside, NASA boffins had enclosed the lander in airbags which automatically inflated at a certain distance from ground level. *Mars Pathfinder* landed at 40 mph, bounced 50 feet, came down, then bounced 15 more times like some bizarre beachball. Eventually it stopped. The airbags deflated. *Mars Pathfinder* opened up like a flower to release "Sojourner," a tiny six-wheeled, robot-controlled vehicle carrying a camera that would take close-up pictures of Martian rocks and anything else of interest it might come upon. "Sojourner" started to roll, then stopped. Its tracks were caught up in one of the deflated airbags.

Over the next two days, NASA scientists on Earth sent signals to the robot in the hope of freeing it. July 6, they succeeded. "Sojourner" broke free and trundled off. From that point until the day contact was lost on September 27, *Mars Pathfinder* returned 2.6 billion bits of information, including more than 16,550 images. The "Sojourner" rover, which was responsible for more than 500 of those pictures, also carried out 15 chemical analyses of rocks and collected data on winds and weather. The lander even managed to complete 83 percent of a 360-degree panned image of the landing site.

NASA pronounced the mission an outstanding success. *Mars Pathfinder*'s lander had operated for nearly three times its design lifetime. "Sojourner" had done even better, exceeding its design spec 12 times over. The billions of bits of information returned by *Mars Pathfinder* and "Sojourner" contained no further evidence of Martian life.

3

THE $154 MILLION *Global Surveyor* was not sabotaged by NASA or shot down by aliens, although it did have trouble with one solar panel. It entered Mars's orbit on September 12, 1997, and began a complicated series of maneuvers designed to place it in the best position for its photographic mission. On March 22, 1998, *Global Surveyor* completed its 202nd orbit and scientists on Earth transmitted commands to activate some of the scientific instruments on board. As the craft hit the low point of each orbit thereafter, data on the Mars atmosphere and gravitational field was collected and cameras were pointed at the Martian surface.

On April 8, 1998, NASA released the first new images of the Cydonia region in more than twenty years. Resolution was roughly ten times that of the old *Viking* photographs. Among the images was a picture of the "Face on Mars" formation, taken in the morning light and from the opposite direction to the originals.

The new picture looked nothing like a human face. "Nothing jumps out at me and screams 'This must have been built by the forces of intelligence,' " commented the *Global Surveyor* camera operations manager dryly. Richard Hoagland reserved judgment. He thought the quality of the latest image was too poor to draw any final conclusion. He was right. When computer enhancement techniques were applied—particularly those that reversed the areas of contrast to simulate the angle of the *Viking* originals—human features began to reappear.

Interestingly, the enhanced *Surveyor* picture looked less like a face in blow-up than it did when reduced. This tended to support the position of those who argued that a mile-long sculpture several million years of age might actually look *less* like a face the closer in you got to it. The same phenomenon is evident in the well-weathered and damaged features of Egypt's Great Sphinx at Giza. No one doubts it has a face, but the closer you get the less evident the features actually become.

Then too, there was the fact that the case for Martian intelligence did not rely on the "Face" alone. There were the other structures at Cydonia to consider and the relationships between them.

Full-scale mapping of the Martian surface—including the Cydonia region—is scheduled to begin in March 1999. It will end on January 31, 2000. Sometime between those dates, we may yet learn the truth about the "Face on Mars."

PHOTO CREDITS

For permission to reproduce copyright photographs, the author and publisher would like to thank the following:

NASA/Science Photo Library	**The Face on Mars**
Mary Evans Picture Library	**Kirlian photography**
e.t. archive	**El Tajin, Veracruz (Mexico)**
Fortean Picture Library	**1,800-year-old battery (Iraq)**
Mary Evans Picture Library	**Map of Atlantis**
Popperfoto/Reuters	**The Cydonia region of Mars**
Mary Evans Picture Library	**Cave painting (Uzbekistan)**
NASA/Science Photo Library	**Mars meteorite**
Barnaby's Picture Library	**The Sphinx**
Fortean Picture Library	**Reconstruction of the Face on Mars**
e.t. archive	**Venus of Willendorf**

INDEX

Aaron, 172
Abihu, 171–72, 177
Abinadab, 179, 180
Abu Ruwash, 67, 105
Abu Simbel, 102–103, 228
Academy of Geneva, 85
Achaeans, 220
Adam (biblical city), 175
Adam (first man), 187
Adan, 80
Adelaide, 80
Advanced technical
  civilizations, 18–19
Aegean, 57
Aerial chariot, 203–204
  see also Aircraft (ancient)
Aeroplane, ancient, 219
  see also Aircraft (ancient)
Africa, 21, 22, 23, 24, 25, 26,
  27, 28, 29, 31, 34, 40, 53, 74,
  92, 118
Agassiz, Louis, 85–86
Ages in Chaos, 153
Agneya, 205
Agriculture, 23
Ahio, 180
Ahura Mazdah, 45
Ai, 176–77
Aigner, Jean S., 184–85
Aircraft (ancient), 203–204,
  207–208, 219
Akhenaten, 99
al-Faiyum, 106
Alabama, 87
Alalush, 224
Alamogordo, 213
Alaska, 57, 79, 89–90, 91, 116
Alexandria, 54, 55, 80
Allen Hills, 16

meteorite, 226
Alpha Centauri, 19, 104
Alps, 79
Altamira, 47, 78
Altiplano, 128
Amalek, 156
Amazon River, 54
Amenhotep III, 101
America, 28, 48, 79, 85, 87,
  218
American Library of Congress,
  53
Ammonites, 43–44
Amsterdam, 80
An-Yang, 100
Anak, 43, 44
Anatolia, 80
Andes, 79, 116, 119, 127
Andesite, 123
Angström Foundation, 9
  Medal, 9
Antikythera, 219
Antarctic, 15, 16, 53–54, 56,
  79, 93, 216
Antares, 104
Antelope Spring, 36
Antwerp, 29, 45
Anuradhapura, 209
Anush, 224
Arabia, 48
Arctic, 90, 91, 93
  Ocean, 90
Ares, 219
Ares Vallis, 230
Argentina, 26, 28, 29, 30, 92
Argolid, 81
Arizona, 13, 42
Arjuna, 202

Ark of the Covenant, 166–67, 168, 169, 170–82
Arkansas, 39
Armstrong, H. L., 36
Artapanus, 156
Ashdod, 178
Ashtoreth, 71
Asia, 22, 23, 71–72, 116
Asia Minor, 220
Assyria, 50
Asteroid, 34
Astronomy, 67–68, 107, 127, 169
Aswan, 55, 102
   Dam, 102
Atharva Veda, 201
Athens, 74, 77, 80
Athens Institute of Seismology, 49
Atlantis, 51–52, 57–59, 64, 81
Atomic Energy Commission, 19
Atomic warfare (ancient), 206
Attica, 81
Aurignacian, 75
Aurillac, 30
Australia, 48, 77
Australopithecus, 22, 184
Austria, 75
Avebury, 73
Ayacucho, 115
Azcapotzalco, 114
Azekah, 176
Aztecs, 114–15, 116
Aztlan, 114

Ba, 147
Bacon, Francis, 52
Barents Sea, 79
Baroda Library, 206
Bashan, 44
Battery (ancient), 138
Battle of Ebenezer, 177
Baumgarten, Martin, 217
Bauval, Robert, 66–67, 68, 70
Behdet, 99
Beijing, 183
Belgium, 28, 29, 30
Belize, 116
Belkov Island, 90
Bellatrix, 67

Bennu bird, 68
Berea College, 35
Bering Strait, 57
Berlin, 12, 84
Bessel, Friedrich, 222
Bethhoron, 176
Bethshemesh, 178, 179
Bhagavad Gita, 201–202
Bibishana, 203
Bible, 71
Biblical Flood, 51, 85, 86
Bingham, Hiram, 133
Bird-soul, 147
   see also Ba
Black Death, 214
Blasket Islands, 2
Block of silver (ancient), 39
Bogotá, 127
Bolan Pass, 210
Bolas, 27
Bolivia, 130
Bolivian altiplano, 121, 126
   see also Altiplano
Bombay, 80
Bonpland, Aimé, 127
Book of Changes, 186
   see also I Ching
Book of Joshua, 174–75
Book of the Dead (Egyptian), 68, 164
Borchardt, Ludwig, 99
Boston, 65
   University, 64
Botswana, 77
Boulder, Colorado, 36
Bragg, Sir William, 197
Brahma Weapon, 206
Brazil, 48, 92
Brera Observatory, 12
Brewster, Sir David, 38
Brisbane, 80
Britain, 38, 45, 92
British Guiana, 92
British Isles, 23
British Museum, 142
Brunton, Dr. Paul, 149–50
Brutus, 45
Buckland, Dr. William, 86
Buddhism, 46
Budge, Sir E. A. Wallis, 159, 161

Buenos Aires, 26
Burma, 30
Burr, Dr. Harold Saxon, 143, 144
Burroughs, Professor W. G., 35
Bushmen, 77
Bushnell, David L., 35

Cairo, 105
   Museum, 63
California, 30, 79
Cambrian, 32
Cambridge Encyclopedia of China, 189
Canaan, 43
Canada, 91
Canals, 13
Canopus, 104
Canton, 190–91
Cape Town, 80
Capella, 104
Capra, Dr. Fritjof, 213–14
Carboniferous, 32, 37, 38, 41
Carlisle, Maurice, 36
Carlotto, Dr. Mark, 3, 6, 7, 216
Carrington, Hereward, 147
Carter, Howard, 168
Carved stone, 38
Casablanca, 80
Catal Huyuk, 73
Caucasus, 79
Cave men, 47
Cayce, Edgar, 52
Celestial Axis, 194
Celestial weapons, 205
Celluloid, 193
Cenozoic, 32
Central America, 52, 118, 119
Cerne Abbas, 45
Ch'ang-yang, 184
Ch'ih Yu, 188
Ch'ing Dynasty, 190–91
Chalcatzingo, 121
Chalk ball, 31
Champollion, Jean François, 101–102
Chang Kwang-chih, 184
Channon, James, 5–6
Chapel of Senusret, 154
Chemistry, 6

Chemosynthesis, 15
Cheops, 106, 161
   Pyramid Razor Blade Sharpener, 146
Chephren, 106
Children of Israel, 151, 167
Children of the Gods, 224
Children of the Sun, 121
Chile, 116
Chimu, 115
China, 23, 26, 27, 48, 50, 183–200
Chou Dynasty, 189
   see also Duke of Chou
Chronus, 45
Chryse Planitia, 14
Chungking, 191
Cicero, 51
Clark, Alvan, 222
Clark, Professor R. T. Rundle, 69
Cleopatra's Needle, 101
Clichy, 25
Colorado, 79
Colossus of Memnon, 101
Columbia
   River, 225
   Union College, 36
Columbus, Christopher, 54
Computer enhancement, 4–5
Concorde, 219
Concrete blocks (ancient), 39
Consensus science, 24, 28–29
Coombs, Dr. Clarence, 36
Copernicus, 222
Cordilleras, 124
Corineus, 44
Cornwall, 44–45
Cortes, Hernan, 114
Costa Rica, 117
Crantor, 51
Cremo, Michael A., 36
Cretaceous, 32, 34, 37
Crete, 50, 52, 220
Critias, 57
Crockall, Robert, 147
Cromer forest bed, 25
Cuba, 54
Cuello, 116–17
Culp, Mrs. S. W., 38

Cumming, Alexander, 213
Cuzco, 115, 121, 131–32, 133, 134–35
Cydonia (Mensae), 1, 5, 7, 9, 14, 40, 113, 215, 216, 228, 230, 232, 233
Czechoslovakia, 22, 142

D&M Pyramid, 7–8, 9
Dagon, 178
Dance of Shiva, 214
Danda, 206
Danube, 78
Dar es Salaam, 80
Dark Ages, 227
Darwin, Charles, 227
Dashur, 106, 108
Daughters of men, 43
David, King, 180, 181
Dead Man, 2
Dean of Westminster, 86
Dearborn Observatory, 222
Dee, Dr. John, 52
Delphi, 100
Demetrius, 71–72
Demi Gods, 208
Deucalion, 82–83
Deuteronomy, 43–44, 158
Devonian, 32, 38
Diana (of the Ephesians), 71–72
Diemos, 33
Digital transmission, 4
Dinosaurs, 17–18, 32, 34–35, 36, 37
Diorite, 63
DiPetro, Vincent, 7
Diring Yurlakh, 27
Discovery program, 230–31
Djhowtey, 170
Dogon, 221–23
Domed colony, 42
Domingo, Frank, 63
Dorset, 45
Douai, 45
Double, 147
Drake, Professor Frank, 2, 3, 18
Drbal, Karel, 146
Druon Antigonus, 45

Dubhe, 104
Dublin, 80
Duke of Chou, 195

East Africa, 21
Ecuador, 116
Eddington, Sir Arthur, 223
Eddy, Professor Robert, 64
Edinburgh, 84
Egg of Chaos, 186
Eggebrecht, Dr. Arne, 138, 139
Egypt, 9, 23, 50, 55, 59–70, 74–75, 77, 81–82, 95–113, 118, 120, 135, 140–42, 146–49, 151, 152, 154, 155–63, 164, 165, 167–68, 181, 185, 187, 208, 210, 212, 218
Einstein, Professor Albert, 84, 93, 94
Eisler, Riane, 72–73, 74
Ekron, 178
El Salvador, 116, 119
El Tajin, 119
Eleazar, 179
Electroplating (ancient), 139
Elizabeth I, Queen, 52
Emims, 43
England, 25, 28, 29, 31, 44, 85, 92, 109, 140
Eocene, 31, 32
Eoliths, 24, 26, 27, 28, 30, 31, 183
Ephesus, 72
Epirus, 220
Eratosthenes, 55, 56
   error, 55, 56
Erh-li-t'ou, 189
Eridanus river, 83
Erjavec, James L., 5
Escape velocity, 33, 41
Ethiopia, 21, 151, 167–68
Études sur les Glaciers, 85
Euboea, 81
Eurasia, 22
Europe, 22, 23, 25, 79, 85, 212, 221
Everest, 87
Exodus, 151, 153, 154, 155–56, 158, 163

Face on Mars, 1, 2, 4–6, 7, 9, 17, 18, 20, 40, 75–76, 228, 230, 232, 233
Faulkner, R. O., 67
Fertile Crescent, 23
Festival of Apet, 168
Fiertek, Robert, 7
First Book of Samuel, 179
First Cataract, 99
Flagstaff, 13
Fluid mechanics, 6
Footprints (ancient), 35–37
Fossil bacteria, 17
Foundation, 182
Fractal
    analysis, 6, 7
    geometry, 6
    mathematics, 6
Fractals, 6
France, 22, 24, 25, 27, 30, 31, 47, 48, 87, 109, 225
Frost, K. T., 49
Fu Hao, 193
Fu-hsi, 187

Gal Oya Dam Project, 209
Galanopoulos, Professor A. G., 49–50
Galileo, 222
Galley Hill, 25
Galvani, Luigi, 137
Gamma Draconis, 104
Gandharva, 205
Gate of the Sun, 122, 129
Gath, 178
Gauri, Dr. K. Lal, 65
Gehe, 26
Genesis, 43, 187, 225
Genetic engineering, 42
Geological Evidence of the Antiquity of Man, 78
Geological Society of London, 86
Geology, 38
Giant's Field, 127, 128
Giants, 43–45
Gibeah, 180
Gibeon, 176
Gilbert, Adrian, 66, 68, 70
Gilmore, Dr. C. W., 35
Ginzberg, Louis, 170

Gittite, 180, 181
Giza, 63, 66, 70, 105, 106, 108, 110, 141, 232
Glen Rose, 36
God, 71, 159, 163–65, 169, 173, 175, 176, 178, 179, 180, 187
Goddess, 71–75, 77, 187, 190, 211
Gog, 45
Gogmagog, 45
Gold chain (ancient), 38, 78
Gold thread (ancient), 38
Golden Age, 45, 47, 70, 220
Golden Calf, 169
Golden Section, 8
Goldin, Daniel, 17
Gómara, Francesco López de, 52
Goths, 97
Grady, Dr. Monica, 17
Great Bath, 211
Great Lion of Tsang-chou, 194
Great Pyramid, 63, 66, 70, 108, 109, 110, 139, 140, 141, 146, 148, 149, 218
Greece, 50, 59, 77, 80, 185
Greek myths, 44
Green, Celia, 147
Green Bank, 18
Greenland, 79, 91
Griaule, Marcel, 221–22
Grolier Electronic Encyclopedia, 97, 168
Guatemala, 116, 117, 119
Guerrero, 117
Gurney, Francis, 147

Hadar, 21
Hadji Ahmed, 57
Hammondville, 38
Hancock, Graham, 164, 167–68
Hanuman, 203
Hapgood, Professor Charles, 53, 54, 55, 56, 57, 77, 80, 92, 93, 94
Harappa, 210–11
Hart, Hornell, 147
Harvard, 98
Hathor, 104
Hatshepsut, 101
Havana, 80

Hawara, 105
  labyrinth, 154
Hawass, Dr. Zahi, 66
Heavener, 39
Hebrew University, 84
Hekau, 163
Helicopter (ancient), 207
Heliopolis, 101
Helios, 83
Helsinki, 80
Hera, 46
Herculaneum, 151
Herodotus, 111
Hesiod, 44, 45, 219, 220
Hesperia, 12
Hexagrams, 188
Heyerdahl, Thor, 121, 209
Hibben, F. C., 90
Hierakonopolis, 61
Hieroglyphic writing, 38, 51
Himalayas, 79, 87, 92
Hindu Kush, 210
Hindu mythology, 46
Hoagland, Richard C., 9, 216, 232
Hodges, Peter, 110–13
Hoffman, Michael, 61–62
Holmes, Arthur, 92–93
Holocene, 24, 32
Holy of Holies, 182
Homer, 185
Hominids, 21, 26
Homo erectus, 22, 26, 27, 184
Homo habilis, 21–22, 27–28, 184
Homo sapiens, 26
Homo sapiens sapiens, 22, 26, 30
Honan, 189
Honduras, 116, 119
Hong Kong, 191
Honorius of Autun, 51
Horeb, 164
Horizon of Khufu, 109
Horus, 158, 165
Horus Kings, 59, 60, 75, 208
Hardec Králové University, 145
Hsia Dynasty, 185, 189
Huang-ti, 188, 189
Huatanay, 132

Hudson Bay, 79
Humboldt, Friedrich von, 127
Hungary, 24
Hutton, James, 86
Huygens, Christian, 222
Hwang Ho valley, 50
Hyatt, John Wesley, 193
Hyksos, 156, 157
Hyperdimensional physics, 9

I Ching, 186, 187, 188, 195
Iamblichus, 51
Ib, 147
Ice Age, 16, 22, 23, 32, 47, 48, 49, 57, 62, 79–81, 85, 86, 89, 90, 91–92, 93, 94, 96, 127, 151
Idaho, 28, 75
Illinois, 37
Illyria, 220
Imhotep, 105
Inca, 114, 115–16, 124, 131–32, 133, 134, 135
Independence Day (U.S. movie), 16
India, 28, 48, 92, 201–209, 210–12, 214
Indra's Dart, 206
Indus, 210
  civilization, 50, 210
Ingalls, Albert G., 38
Inis Tuaisceart, 2, 3
Interstellar travel, 19–20
International Academy of Sanskrit Research, 207
Iowa, 38
Ipswich, 25
Ipuwer, 152–53, 155
Iran, 45
Iraq Museum, 138
Ireland, 2, 85
Isis, 70, 104
Israel, 43, 169, 175, 176, 179, 180
Istanbul, 53, 80
Italy, 27, 28, 29, 80
Ivory Coast, 53

Japan, 48, 77
Java, 26
Jeep, 6

Jehovah, 164
Jericho, 175, 176
Jerusalem, 180, 181
JHVH, 164
Jordan, 174–75
Josephus, 158
Joshua, 44, 174–77, 178
Josyer, G. R., 207
*Journal of the American
  Society for Psychical
  Research*, 147
Jupiter, 33–34, 84, 222
Jupiter's bolts, 137
Jura Mountains, 85
Jurassic, 32, 37

Ka, 147
  see also Out-of-body
  experience
Kalasasaya, 122, 129–30
Kanam, 27
Kanjera, 25
Kansu, 196
Karachi, 80, 210–11
Karnak, 103, 104, 154
Kayappia, 123
Keene State College, 54
Kentucky, 35
Kenwood, Frank J., 39
Kenya, 25, 27, 29, 30
Khafre, 63, 106
Khufu, 63, 106, 108, 109, 110,
  148, 161
King's chamber, 66, 108, 141,
  149
Kingoodie Quarry, 38
Kingston, 80
Kiriathjearim, 179
Kirlian, Semyon Davidovich,
  143–44
Kirlian photography, 144
Kitchen, Kenneth, 168
Kittyhawk, 206
König, Wilhelm, 138, 139
Korea, 48
Kosmas, 51
Koyukuk, 90
Krishna, 202, 205
Krita Yuga, 46
Krmessky, Dr. Julius, 145
Kung-kung, 187

Kurukshetra, 202
Kuskokwim River, 90
Kwazulu, 45

La Venta, 117, 119–20
Lacahahuira, 126
Lacovara, Peter, 65
Lacquer, 193
Laka Kollu, 122
Lake Coipasa, 126
Lake Minchin, 128
Lake Texcoco, 114
Lake Titicaca, 121, 126, 127,
  128, 131
Landsburg, Alan, 122–23
Lanka, 202, 204, 208, 209
  see also Sri Lanka
Leakey, Louis, 21, 25, 27
Lebanon, 217–18
Legends of the Jews, 170
Lehner, Dr. Mark, 66
Leibniz, Gottfried Wilhelm
  von, 186
Leiden Papyrus, 152, 155, 156
Lethbridge, Tom C., 224, 225
Levites, 172, 177, 179
Leviticus, 158, 171
Leyden jar, 140
Liakhov Islands, 90
Library of Alexandria, 54
Light-penetrating mirrors,
  196–97
Lima, 80
Liu-chiang, 184
Lockyer, Sir Norman, 100,
  103–104
London, 80, 142, 196, 213
Lord's Song, 202
Los Angeles, 80
Los Angeles Times, 65
Lowell, Percival, 13
Lung Shan, 185
Lung-Hsi, 196
Luxor, 104, 167
Lyell, Sir Charles, 78, 86, 96

Ma-pa, 184
Macedonia, 220
Machu Picchu, 132–35
Macoupin County, 37
Madagascar, 92

Magog, 45
Mahabharata, 201, 202, 204–205
Maharshi Bharadawaja, 207
Mahawamsa, 209
Makkedah, 176
Mallery, Alington H., 53–54, 56
Mammoths, 89, 90–91, 227
Man in the Moon, 2, 3
Manco Capac, 115, 121
Manetho, 59–60, 208
Marcellus, 51
Marco Polo, 190
Mariette, Auguste, 101
Mariner IV, 13
Mars, 1, 4, 7, 10–14, 16–18, 20, 23, 31, 33, 37, 40–41, 42–43, 52, 58, 215–16, 226, 228–33
    Mission, 9
    Mars Observer, 230
Martian meteorites, 15–17, 216
    Martian atmosphere, 16
    Martian civilization, 217
    Martian climate, 17
    Martian equator, 11
    Martian rock, 16
    Martian temperature, 10
    Martian year, 10
Marseilles, 80
Martinatos, Professor S., 49
Maryland, 36
Massachusetts, 13
Mastaba, 105
Mathis, Atlas Almon, 39
Mausala Parva, 206
Maya, 116, 117, 118–19
Maydum, 106
McDaniel, Professor Stanley V., 1, 2, 216, 217
McGill, G. E., 5
McKinley, James, 226
Mecca, 100
Mediterranean, 22, 55, 74, 98, 99
Mehrgarh, 210
Meister, William J., 36, 37
Melbourne, 80
Memphis, 61, 99
Memphis Serapeum, 101
Menes, 60, 61, 120

Mentuhotep II, 106
Mercator Projection, 54
Mercer, Samuel B., 67
Merneptah, 153
Mesoamerica, 23, 50, 114, 116, 117, 121, 211, 221
Mesopotamia, 50, 210, 220–21
Mesozoic, 32, 34
Metal nail (ancient), 38, 78
Mexico, 48, 114, 119, 127
Michigan, 87
Microscopic life forms, 16
Mid-Atlantic Ridge, 53
Middle Kingdom, 46
Midi, 30
Midian, 159, 163, 174
Milan, 12
Militha, 204
Milky Way, 18, 67
Milliard, Dr. Douglas, 17
Minchin, J. B., 128
Minoan Crete, 49–50, 72, 73–74
Minoan hypothesis, 49–50
Miocene, 29, 30, 32
Missouri, 35
Moabites, 43
Moche, 119
Mohenjo-daro, 210–12, 214
Molenaar, 7
Monte Hermoso, 26
Montevideo, 80
Moons, 33
Morocco, 53
Morrisonville, 38
Moscow, 84, 142
Moscow News, 36
Moscow University, 15
Moses, 43, 44, 157–61, 163–67, 169–71, 173, 174, 175, 176, 178, 181
Moulin Quignon, 25
Mount Ebal, 176
Mount Everest, 87
Mount Gerizim, 100
Mount McKinley, 89
Mount Moriah, 181
Mount of Vision, 181
Mount Sinai, 154, 172
Muldoon, Sylvan, 147–48
Müller, Dr. Rolf, 130, 134–35

Museum of Fine Arts (Boston), 65
Mycenaeans, 220
Myers, Frederick, 147
Mysore, 207
Myth, 43–46

Nabian Pluvial, 65, 69
Nadab, 171–72, 177
Nagas, 208
Namibia, 48
Nampa, 28, 75, 78
Napoleon, 109
NASA, 1, 2, 4, 10, 15, 16, 17, 18, 217, 230, 231, 232
National Geographic Society, 133
National Radio Astronomy Observatory, 18
Natural History Museum (London), 16, 17
Natural Science Museum (London), 17
Neanderthals, 22–23
Near East, 23, 221
Needham, Dr. Joseph, 191–92, 199–200
Nefertari, 102
Neoliths, 24, 29, 30
Neoplatonism, 51
New Hampshire, 3, 54
New Jersey, 215
New Mexico, 213
New Siberian Islands, 90
New World, 50, 52, 119
New York, 9, 80
    Police Department, 63
New York Times, 66
New Zealand Alps, 79
Nigeria, 226
Nile, 55, 59, 60, 61, 62, 95, 96, 103, 105, 118, 141, 151, 152, 185
Nilometer, 151
Noah, 82
Noah's Ark, 82
Norse sagas, 44
North America, 79, 88
North Pole, 52, 57
Nü-Kua, 186–87

Nubia, 154
Numbers, 43, 158, 173

Oaxaca Valley, 121
Obededom, 180, 181
Occult Japan, 13
Og, 44
Ohio, 38
Oklahoma, 39
Old Europe, 220
Old Man of the Mountain, 3
Old Testament, 43, 71, 153, 156, 158, 159, 161, 163, 168, 180–81, 187
Old World, 23
Olduvai, 21, 22, 25, 27
Oligocene, 30, 32
Ollantaytambu, 135
Olmec, 117–18, 119–21, 124, 218
Olympus, 44, 46, 224
Olympus Mons, 11
Omphalos, 99
Open University, 16
Opium Wars, 191
Ordovician, 32
Orichalcum, 57, 58
Orion, 66–67, 68, 70, 104, 146
Orion Mystery, 66
Orion's Belt, 66, 67
Oronteus Finaeus, 56
Osiris, 68, 70, 139, 165
Ostrander, Sheila, 142–43, 144
Out-of-body experience, 147–50

P'an-ku, 186
Pacific Northwest Laboratory, 226
Pakashana, 206
Pakistan, 28, 211
Paleocene, 32
Paleontology, 35
Paleozoic, 32
Palenque, 119
Paleoliths, 24, 25, 27, 28, 29, 30, 31, 184
Palermo, 80
Palestine, 23, 84
Paluxy River, 36, 37
Panama Canal, 88

Pandava, 205
Pangaea, 92
Paris, 87, 225
Parnassus, 82
Parsons, James, 38
Patagonia, 48
Pathfinder, 230–31
Paul the Apostle, 71
Pavlita, Robert, 145–46, 148
Peking man, 183
Peloponnese, 81
Pennsylvania, 35
Pepi II, 106
Perizzites, 44
Permian, 32, 92
Persian Gulf, 23
Perth, 80
Peru, 48, 115, 130, 131, 221
Petrie, Sir Flinders, 108, 142
Phact, 104
Phaethon, 83
Phantasms of the Living, 147
*Phenomena of Astral
     Projection,* 147
Phidias, 78
Philistines, 177–78, 180
Philo, 158, 159
Phobos, 33
Phoenix, 68, 69
Photoclinometry, 3
Photomicrographs, 36
Photosynthesis, 14
Phthia, 82
Physiology, 6
Pillars of Hercules, 47, 49–50
Piri Re'is, 53–55, 56
Pizarro, Franciso, 114
Placer County, 30
Plato, 47, 49, 50, 51, 52, 57,
     58, 59, 74, 77, 81
Platon, Nicolas, 72
Platonic Academy, 51
Pleistocene, 24, 28, 32, 47, 75,
     77, 79, 87, 89, 95, 185
Pliocene, 24, 28, 29, 32, 128
Podmore, Frank, 147
Pompeii, 151
Poōpo, 126
Port au Prince, 80
Portolans, 54
Portugal, 30, 48

Poseidon, 57
Poseidonios, 51
Posnansky, Arthur, 129–30,
     134
Potassium, 11
Poynton, John, 147
Praxiteles, 78
Precession of the equinoxes,
     68–69
Precessional motion, 68–69
Press Trust of India, 207
Principles of Geology, 86
Proclus, 51
Project Ozma, 18
Projection, 147
Psychotronic generators, 144
Psychotronics, 142–45
Ptolemy I, 54
Pulkovo Observatory, 12
Punjab, 211
Purcell, Edward, 19
Pushpaka, 203
Putuni, 122
Pyramid of the Sun, 119
Pyramid Texts, 67, 70
"Pyramidiots," 141
Pyrenees, 47
Pyrrha, 82

Q'eri Kala, 122
Qadesh, 169
Quantum physics, 202
Quebec, 80
Queen's chamber, 66

Rabat, 80
Race of bronze, 219–20
Race of silver, 219
Rama, 203–204, 208
Ramayana, 201, 202–204, 205–
     206, 208
Rameses II, 102, 103, 153, 228
Randi, James, 148
Ravana, 206
Red Sea, 161
Redmount, Carol, 65
Reincarnation, 22
Rejdak, Dr. Zdenek, 144
Renaissance, 96
Reykjavik, 80
Richmond, 226

Rig Veda, 201
Rio de Janeiro, 80
River Maule, 116
River Tweed, 38
Robinson, John Mansley, 219
Rockcastle County, 35, 37
Rome, 50
Royal Engineers, 110
Russia, 12

Sabu, Prince, 218
Sacred geometry, 9
Sacsahuaman, 132
Sagan, Professor Carl, 215, 216
Saiph, 67
Sais, 59, 84, 95
Sakkara, 66
Sama Veda, 201
Samothrace, 80
San Lorenzo, 117, 120
Santorini, 49
Saqqara, 67, 101, 105, 218, 219
Sargon, King, 158
Sastry, Subbaraya, 207
Sastry, Venkatrama, 207
Saussure, Horace Bénédict de, 85
Sautuola, Marcelino Sanz de, 47–48
Schiaparelli, Giovanni Virginio, 12–13
Schoch, Professor Robert, 64, 65, 66
Schroeder, Lynn, 142–43, 144
Science and Civilisation in China, 191–92
Science Museum, 196
Scientific consensus, 34
Scotland, 57, 85, 86
Scripta Universitatis atque Bibliothecae Hierosolymitarum, 84
Search for Extra Terrestrial Intelligence, 18
Second body, 148
  see also Ka
Seismograph (ancient), 196
Semneh, 151
Seneferu, 162, 163
Set, 165

SETI, 18
Seven Seas, 88
Shang
  dynasty, 183, 184, 185–86, 189, 192, 193
  civilization, 50
Shanghai, 80
Shebarim, 177
Shen-nung, 187–88
Shensi, 187
Shetiyyah, 182
Shoe print (fossilized), 36–37
Shun, 189
Siberia, 27, 57, 91, 116
Sicily, 48
Siemens, Sir William, 139–41
Silurian, 32
Sinai, 164
Sirius, 66, 69–70, 104, 222
Sirius B, 222, 223
Sky People, 223
SLMEs, 226
Smithsonian, 35
Snefru, 67, 106, 108, 161
Soan Valley, 28
Sobekneferure, 154
Society for Psychical Research, 147
Sojourner, 231
Solar Weapon, 206
Solomon, 71, 181, 182
Solon, 59, 81, 82, 95
Sons of God, 43, 225
South America, 50, 53, 88, 121, 124, 127, 131, 218
South Pole, 56
Southeast Asia, 221
Southward-pointing carriage, 195–96
Soviet Union, 143, 145
Space Biology Laboratory, 15
Spain, 25
Sphinx, 63–66, 232
Spitsbergen, 91
Sri Lanka, 204, 208–209
St. Prest, 27
Stall, Jim, 39
Star Trek, 215
Stecchini, Professor Livio Catullo, 97–98, 99, 100
Stein, Michael C., 6

Step Pyramid, 105
Stevens, Todd, 226
Stockholm, 80
Stolbovoi Island, 90
Stonehenge, 73
Strabo, 101
Strange fire, 172
Studies of Glaciers, 85
Subsurface Lithoautotrophic
  Microbial Ecosystem, 226
Sulphur Springs, 39
Sumaria, 227, 228
Sunspots, 194–95
Surveyor, 230, 231–32
Switzerland, 31
Sydney, 80
Syene, 55, 99
Syrian Desert, 23
Syrianus, 51

Table Mountain, 30
Tacoma, 36
Tanana Valley, 89
Tanzania, 21, 25, 27
Tasmania, 79
Tchatcha-em-ankh, 161–63
Tel Aviv, 80
Temple, Robert G., 192, 193–
  94, 199
Temple of Amon-Ra, 103
Temple of the Sun, 132, 135
Ten Commandments, 164
Tenochtitlan, 114–15
Teotihuacan, 119
Terra Amata, 24
Texas, 36
Thames Embankment, 101
Thasos, 80
The Geologist, 37
The Sign and the Seal, 164
The Times, 38
Thebes, 99, 101
Thessaly, 80, 82
Thomas, 39
Thompson, Richard L., 36
Thorium, 11
Thoth, 164, 170
Thutmose, 101
Tiahuanaco, 121–26, 128–31,
  134, 135, 136, 216
Timaeus, 59

Timbuktu, 79
Tired Stone, 134
Titicaca, 121, 126, 129
Tlatelolco, 114
Tokyo, 80
Toltecs, 119
Topkapi Palace museum, 53
Toron, Erol, 7–8
Toronto University, 67
Torralba, 25
Tres Zapotes, 121
Triassic, 32, 34, 37
Trigrams, 187, 188
Trimble, Virginia, 66
Trinil, 26
Tropic of Cancer, 99
Trouvelot, E. L., 12
Troy, 220
Tullumayo River, 132
Turin Papyrus, 60, 75
Turkey, 30, 53, 142
Turkmen Republic, 36, 37
Tutankhamen, 168

USSR, 36
Ulalinkla, 27
UNESCO, 102
Uniformitarianism, 86, 88–89,
  96, 227–28
United States Navy
  Hydrographic Office, 53
University of California, 65
University of Chicago, 66
University of Colorado, 36
University of New Mexico, 90
University of Vienna, 213
Upanishads, 201
Urals, 79
Uranium, 11
Ursa Major, 104
Urubamba Valley, 132
Utah, 36
Utopia Planitia, 14
Uyuni, 126
Uzzah, 180

Val d'Arno, 27
Valmiki, 202
Vancouver, 80
Vedas, 201
Vega, Garcilasco de la, 134

Velikovsky, Immanuel, 83–85, 151, 152, 153–55, 156, 157, 159, 161
Venus, 84, 85, 222
Venus of Willendorf, 75
Veracruz, 117, 119
Vértesszöllös, 24
Vesica piscis, 8
Vienna, 84
Vijaya, 208, 209
Viking photographs, 1, 2–5, 14, 232
Viking I, 1, 14
Viking II, 1, 14
Vikings, 97
Vilcabamba, 133
Viracocha, 121, 129
Virgil, 45
Virginis, 19
Volta, Alessandro, 137
Völuspá, 46
Von Daniken, Erich, 19, 52, 224, 225
Vyas, Kunwarlal Jain, 208
Vyasa, 201
Vymaanika-Shaastra, 207

Wall (ancient), 39
Walters, M. I., 53
Wandjina, 223
War of the Worlds, 215
Washington (State), 225, 226
Water closet, 213
Weathering, 64–65
Webster City, 38
Wegener, Alfred, 92
Welles, Orson, 215
Wellington, 80
West, John Anthony, 62–64
West Virginia, 18
Western Australia, 17
Whales, 87–89
Wheeler, Sir Mortimer, 210, 214, 217

White dwarf, 223
Wilburton Mine, 39
Willendorf, 75
    Venus, 78
World Ocean, 88
World War Two, 110, 191
Worlds in Collision, 84, 153
Wright Brothers, 206

Xihoudu, 27, 184

Yahweh, 163, 170
Yajur Veda, 201
Yakkhas, 208, 209
Yale University, 64, 184
    Peruvian Expeditions, 133
    School of Medicine, 143
Yang Shao culture, 185
Yao, 189
Yaweh, 164
Yellow Emperor, 188, 189, 190, 200
Yellow River, 183, 185
Yu-hsiung, 189–90
Yuanmou, 27
Yuanmou man, 183, 184
Yucatan, 116
Yugas, 46
Yugoslavia, 22, 80
Yukon, 90

Zaire, 48
Zamzummims, 44
Zaretan, 175
Zawyat al Aryan, 67
Zeus, 46, 82, 83
Zidonians, 71
Zimbabwe, 48
Zoroaster, 45
Zoser, 105, 106, 108
Zürich, 84

ABOUT THE AUTHOR

HERBIE BRENNAN is the author of more than sixty works of fact and fiction, with combined sales now well in excess of seven million copies. As a writer he has never been shy of dealing with controversial subject matter, and his subjects have included out-of-body experiences and time travel. Herbie Brennan has broadcast and lectured throughout the U.S. and Europe. He lives in Ireland.